Grandfathered

Praise for *Grandfathered*

"Grandparenthood is the most important period in our lives. Hard-won life lessons are a priceless legacy to the next generation, and in passing them on, we are rewarded with nonjudgmental, unconditional love. Ian Haysom's delightful vignettes take us through the increasing number and ages of his brood of grandchildren and elicit chuckles, nods, and tears."

David Suzuki

"I must admit I was quite worried about Ian's retirement. What would he do without news anchor egos to soothe? But I think he's really found his calling as 'Grandad.' There is pure joy in his words about Mayana, Emma, and Linden ... and his whole family, come to think of it. Ian's writing is full of love and humour and wonder at the miracle of grandparenthood. *Grandfathered* is such a pleasure to read—even for someone who has no children or grandchildren. This book is a gift his grandkids will treasure forever."

Sophie Lui anchor, *Global BC News Hour*

"Baby Boomers don't like the word 'old.' They prefer 'classic' instead. Classic Rock, classic movies, classic cars. This book is about a new way to look at the old—sorry, *classic*—members of a family. It's true that today's grandparent is nothing like past grandparents. Just as someone once pointed out that 70 is the new 60, and 60 is the new 50, and 50 is the new 40, and so on, Ian Haysom has shown us that grandfather is the new cool uncle."

Squire Barnes TV personality, *Global BC*

"I couldn't put it down. A gifted writer that I read religiously in the *Times Colonist*, Ian Haysom has delivered a gem with *Grandfathered*. I'm not a grandfather, but as Ian points out in the book, 'Grandchildren always laugh at your jokes.' So for that reason alone, I hope I become one soon!"

Ed Bain host of *The Q Morning Show* at 100.3 The Q!
and CHEK TV Victoria Weather Guy

"Written with the sure hand and wandering eye of a veteran journalist, *Grandfathered* lives somewhere between heartfelt memoir and hilarious instruction manual. Ian Haysom has written one of the most thoroughly charming page-turners I've ever had the pleasure to read. You're going to enjoy this book, and you'll be surprised how many times it makes you laugh out loud or moves you to tears ... often on the same page."

Ian Ferguson author of *The Survival Guide to British Columbia* and winner of the Stephen Leacock Medal for Humour for *Village of the Small Houses*

"We are all suckers for a good love story, which is what Ian Haysom has written here. He has a deceptively light touch, wry and cheerful, while finding insight in little human moments that will leave even non-grandparents nodding their heads in recognition."

Jack Knox Stephen Leacock Medal–nominated author of
Hard Knox: Musings from the Edge of Canada and *Opportunity Knox:
Twenty Years of Award-Losing Humour Writing*

"Ian Haysom has written a humorous, touching, and engaging meditation on what it means to be a grandfather. His skillful storytelling, powerful prose, and thoughtful insights had me laughing and thinking, often at the same time. While I'm not quite yet a grandfather myself, I feel so much better prepared in the wake of this fine and funny book."

Terry Fallis two-time winner of the
Stephen Leacock Medal for Humour

Ian Haysom

Grandfathered

Dispatches from the Trenches
of Modern Grandparenthood

Heritage House Publishing Company Ltd.
heritagehouse.ca

Cataloguing information available from Library and Archives Canada

978-1-77203-333-5 (pbk)
978-1-77203-334-2 (ebook)

Edited by Warren Layberry
Cover and interior design by Jacqui Thomas
Excerpts from columns appearing on pages 12–14 and 94–96 are reproduced with
permission from the Victoria *Times Colonist*.

The interior of this book was produced on 100% post-consumer recycled paper,
processed chlorine free, and printed with vegetable-based inks.

Heritage House gratefully acknowledges that the land on which we live and work
is within the traditional territories of the Lkwungen (Esquimalt and Songhees),
Malahat, Pacheedaht, Scia'new, T'Sou-ke, and W̱SÁNEĆ (Pauquachin, Tsartlip,
Tsawout, Tseycum) Peoples.

We acknowledge the financial support of the Government of Canada through the
Canada Book Fund (CBF) and the Canada Council for the Arts, and the Province
of British Columbia through the British Columbia Arts Council and the Book
Publishing Tax Credit.

24 23 22 21 20 1 2 3 4 5

Printed in Canada

"I know what heaven is. Heaven is my granddaughter, who lives next door, playing in the street with her friends. When I see that, that's heaven. I don't think heaven can be better than that."

Clive James
writer and broadcaster, shortly before his death

"There are fathers who do not love their children; there is no grandfather who does not adore his grandson."

Victor Hugo

Contents

Introduction

We are not our grandfather.

We are Grandpa and Grandad and Bubba and Gramps. But we are not our grandfather.

We are twenty-first century grandfathers, baby boomers who never really grew up and still haven't quite figured out how to be parents, let alone grandparents.

Our grandfathers had World Wars and Frank Sinatra and Charlie Chaplin. We had Vietnam and the Beatles and Jimi Hendrix and Robert Redford (who we are kind of happy to see is beginning to look his age, meaning he's human too).

Right. We are not our grandfather.

Not in our heads anyway. The stereotype of the grandfather is a white-haired, kindly old man who wears slippers and sits his grandchildren on his knee and has a wrinkly smile. That's not what we see. We still see ourselves as vibrant, useful, relevant participants in the world. Then again, that's probably not what our grandchildren see. They see white-haired, kindly old men. They have better eyesight than us.

We are going to live longer than our grandfathers too. If we are lucky enough to live in parts of Asia, Western Europe, Oceania, or North America, we might live well into our eighties and beyond. We'll likely get to know our grandchildren a lot longer and a whole lot better than our grandfathers knew us. If we live in other parts of the world, where the life expectancy for men hovers between the mid-fifties and mid-sixties, then we may not make it to the weathered shores of

Grandfatherland. Still, across the globe, people today are living twice as long as they were in 1900.

And, on average, we're a whole lot healthier. Most of us don't smoke. We eat more wisely than our grandfathers. We kayak and ski and run and play tennis (or pickleball) and curl and play golf and we ride bikes, even if some of them are battery powered.

This book is about being a grandfather in the twenty-first century—and also about being a father. I have included a few favourite newspaper columns I wrote about being a twentieth-century dad. To be a grandfather you usually had to be a father first. So, you know, we've got some experience.

Despite the angry, sometimes helpless and hopeless world we seem to live in these days, with all the chaos and fake news around us and all the noise, this is a mostly optimistic book. Because, simply, children are the future. They still have innocence; they still have hope. And we grandfathers, often sidelined in the past, suddenly have a more important role to play. Even if that role is telling bad jokes and picking our grandkids up when they fall down.

I was in the changing room at the gym the other day (WARNING: modern grandad story) and an older chap hailed a younger guy.

"Hey, how's it going? Haven't seen you in a while."

"Well, that's because I'm a new dad. I've been a bit busy."

"That's fantastic. Congratulations," said the older man. "Boy or girl?"

"A girl. She's three, no, four weeks old."

"Beautiful," said the old man. "A new girl. And new hope for the future. Maybe she's going to be the one who finds a cure for cancer."

I smiled at that. Maybe she will, maybe she won't. But the old man was right. Where there's life, there's hope. And where there's new life, there's magic in the air.

Especially when you're a grandfather.

What you're about to read is a journey through grandfatherhood, from baby steps (theirs and mine) through to a kind of grandfatherly maturity. Ten years of thoughts, reflections, and memories,

2

collected in the shoeboxes of my mind over this past decade. A bit of a jumble, perhaps, but that's where we store our memories.

And just for fun, because this is not *all* about me, I asked some of my friends who are also grandads or grandpas to send me some anecdotes or thoughts on being a grandfather, and they are contained in this book. Some are hilarious. Some joyful. My very good friend, Donald, who is a pediatrician in Scotland, emailed me his contribution with the following addition: "Ian seems keen on coincidences—he's especially keen on the apparent coincidence that his first grandchild is the best granddaughter ever and apparently she also has the best grandfather ever!"

That's true of just about every grandfather. There have been grandparents beyond count before us, and there will be countless more after we're gone, but all grandfathers have had—and will have—one thing in common: they all believe theirs are the best of grandkids.

Donald also makes note of the fact that every time he's with his grandchildren he can't stop smiling. I know what he means.

Enjoy this book if you're a grandfather, a grandmother, a grandkid or somewhere in between. I hope you find yourself in here somewhere. And smile some. •

1. Becoming a Grandfather

The week that my first grandchild, Mayana, was born, I wrote this diary entry:

SATURDAY: I am on Salt Spring Island watching two first-time, very young-looking grandmothers cooing and laughing and giving beaming smiles to a one-day-old girl without a name. One of these grandmothers is my wife, Beth.

I call the child, temporarily, Molly, until her parents stop dithering and pick a name for this little wonder. By week's end she will be Mayana.

My daughter is beautiful, glowing as she cradles her first child. The child's father looks proud and happy. The sun is shining and a beam of light falls on the baby's face. She blinks a little and then opens her eyes wide and looks around at us, her new family. Her besotted, beaming family.

In our lives, our journeys begin as babies, as sons or daughters, as brothers or sisters, then as husbands and wives and partners, then, perhaps, as mothers or fathers, uncles or aunts, then, if we're lucky, as grandparents.

Each of us playing our part.

Today, for the first time, I am a grandfather. Another new role.

My wife looks down at the child. "You are surrounded by so much love." She got that right. May it ever be so.

Mayana—pronounced My-Anna—was born at home on Salt Spring on a beautiful winter wonderland of a day in January. My daughter Amy had a midwife, a partner, and her mother to help out. It was all very Salt Spring–alternative. Candles and meditative music and water and calm. Well, it was supposed to be, but the electricity failed and they couldn't heat the water that was needed for some kind of spiritual immersion bath, and the candles, far from offering a special atmosphere, failed to provide enough light, so there was much frantic rushing around, and Amy, who was supposed to be in a sort of yoga-calm-Om kind of state, after one severe contraction, let out a loud, primal yell.

Also, I had baked a blackberry pie for after the birth because it was Amy's favourite. She had put it in the freezer. Where it was left, forgotten, when the business of giving birth arrived. In one of Amy's final, intense contractions, just before her baby arrived, she let out another primal howl and then turned to Beth.

"Mum, quick, get the pie out of the freezer."

She knew she was close. And ready for pie.

I wasn't there, but in Vancouver at work, which in hindsight was probably a good thing. The other young-looking grandmother mentioned was Lakhi. She and I got on a very slow ferry and were there to bill and coo and feel like a billion dollars within a few hours. It was a magical time.

Mayana did that little thing with her mouth when I first saw her, pouting and popping her lips, probably looking for food like a little bird, but—oh my—did she look wonderful. Lots of dark hair and dark eyes, and light brown skin, a mix of Caucasian and Indian. I immediately felt a bond with her. And wanted to hug her. And did.

Home births were nothing new to our family. Both our sons, Tim and Paul, were born at our small blue home in West Vancouver in the eighties. Midwifery was not totally accepted in North America in those days; it resided in a sort of legal grey area. Today it's much more common. And legal. We had a super midwife and a supportive doctor. And my wife felt strongly about a natural home birth.

Both our daughters, Amy and Jani, were born in Ottawa, at Grace Hospital, which was fine, if somewhat antiseptic. I was there for both births, and they were very efficient, and I did my supportive coach/husband thing very well, if I say so myself, and didn't faint. My wife had no complaints, but her feelings at the time were clear enough.

"I don't know why I'm in a hospital to give birth. I'm not exactly sick."

I must admit, I did disgrace myself at Amy's birth when Beth was being wheeled into the delivery room.

"It's okay," I said. "You can back out now if you like."

There was much laughter from the nurses. "Bit late for that sweetheart," one of them said.

Oh no, I tried to explain, I meant she could have an epidural if she wanted, she didn't have to feel like a failure or anything, but I was drowned out by laughter, and now it's part of family folklore, and I'm an idiot, which is the natural order of things.

When it came to baby number three, Beth said she'd like to explore the idea of a home birth. We'd emigrated from England in the early seventies where midwives were common and a crucial part of the health system (just check out the BBC's *Call the Midwife*) and we were comfortable and confident that all would be okay. And it was.

Beth delivered Tim, and within an hour or so, we were all at home together and it all felt, well, natural. Ditto with Paul. So when Amy said she'd like to have Mayana at home, she came by it honestly. Even in Canada, it's not so unusual anymore.

And my wife was right. Mayana was, in her first few days on the planet, surrounded by so much love.

By her besotted, beaming family.

Pure. And simple. And perfect. •

My Grandparents

Becoming a grandparent, of course, naturally casts one's mind back to their own grandparents. We remember them, usually with unquestioning affection. They are part of the furniture of our lives, comfortable sofas that we often jumped on, as they smiled at us and cuddled us and mussed our hair.

We had no expectations of them, except to be there. And even if they lived a long way away, which is more usual these days, we knew they'd come to us with gifts and hugs and wrinkles and huge smiles. Because a grandfather and a grandmother were more special than just about anything.

And they let us get away with murder. Or at least we got to do things and eat things—mostly chocolate—that our parents wouldn't let us. Plus ça change.

I had two grandfathers but never knew my paternal grandfather. He died when I was a baby (as did my paternal grandmother). And my father never spoke about him. I recently asked my stepbrother, sixteen years my senior, why that should be.

"He was very strict towards Dad," he said. "I don't think Dad had the happiest childhood at home."

My mother's dad, my grandad, was also strict. With his own children, that is. But not towards me or my sisters. He was a Yorkshireman who served in the army in India in the First World War. He was a small, wiry man, Tom Edwards. Or "our Tom" as my grandmother—Nan or Nanny—used to call him.

They lived in a terraced house on Mersey Street in Hull, like a location right out of *Coronation Street*, with an outside lavatory—the lav—and newspapers cut into small squares for toilet paper. Going to the toilet in winter was an uncomfortable and scratchy ordeal.

There was no bath. Only a sink in which to strip wash. The only sink in the house was in the small kitchen, or scullery. My grandfather would wash and shave there and comb his hair in front of a tiny mirror, sometimes cracking jokes at me.

"You'll be shaving soon, lad. You should start with the top of your head."

A small tin bath was sometimes moved into the middle of the back room, in front of a coal fire. I never knew where my grandad bathed, though the local swimming pool—or slipper baths—offered baths for three pennies.

My grandparents were proudly working class. My grandad, in a flat cap, went out to work as a warehouseman in a factory. My grandmother always worked in the home, scurrying around my grandad, cooking his meals, making his tea. In all the time I knew him, he never once cooked a meal or made a drink. Men didn't do that.

The past is another country. They do things differently there.

I spent a lot of time with my grandparents, even though I lived then in the south of England, and they in the north. I would head to their house with my sister for summer holidays, sometimes a month at a time. I loved being there. It was very different from my own relatively modern suburban life. Grittier, more real in many ways. Hull was a fishing port, and there was a fish-and-chip shop on just about every street. My nan would routinely send me out to pick up fish and chips wrapped in newspaper. Or, more often, patty and chips—a sort of battered fishcake. I only discovered recently there was no fish in the patty. So I was eating battered potato and fried potato. Hmmm ... no wonder I loved dinners there. Vegetables were a rumour. Mushy peas were a luxury.

I remember my grandad with absolute affection. He was always generous to me. Sometimes, when I left for home, he'd pull a shiny half-crown—two shillings and sixpence—out of his pocket and put it in my hand.

"Go and buy yourselves some treats, lad."

It was a fortune and I treasured my fortune.

He was a fan of rugby league and, more specifically, Hull Kingston Rovers, the local team within walking distance of his house. He took me to see them a few times when I was seven or eight years old, but he had a word of advice that has stayed with me ever since.

"Watching sports is for old men and cripples," he said. "While you can play you *should* play."

I still feel guilty lying on a sofa watching hockey or soccer. But I still go out and play, albeit badly.

He also took me to see a cricket test match, an international between England and Australia. We travelled on a bus—or coach, as we called it in England—to Leeds together for two hours either way. On the way home the men trooped into a pub, and I sat outside. My grandad brought me an orange juice and a bag of crisps and sat with me on a bench. The day had been thrilling, magical, exotic. Inside, the men were singing songs, and I looked up at him.

"Nice day, lad?"

"Smashing," I said.

He died when I was fourteen. He went upstairs for an afternoon nap and never woke up. He was only sixty-four. My nan never got over losing him, and she lived to ninety-nine. He was her one and only true love. "Our Tom."

When I think of my grandad, I realize all he had to do to be special to me was to be there. Sitting in his armchair in the corner of the room, his eyes twinkling as he looked at me, ruffling my hair every time he walked past me. We romanticize our childhoods. And that's as it should be. Our grandparents should be part of the furniture of our lives. Very comfortable. And very old.

There was one moment, when I was about thirteen, that I felt embarrassed. I saw my grandfather coming home from work, trudging along the long street. He was wearing his work clothes, including a hat and a tie and a somewhat shabby jacket. Men in those days always wore ties. It was part of who they were. I meanwhile was dressed in a T-shirt and sky-blue jeans, which were fashionable at the time. I hadn't seen my grandfather in some time, but he looked old (he was only in his early sixties) and worn and I felt silly and somewhat shabby and disreputable in these new sky-blue jeans. Incongruous perhaps. And, worse, I was almost as tall as Grandad.

"All right, son?" he asked, and gave my arm a squeeze. Then he looked at my jeans. "You look a right dandy in those." He gave me a smile, nonetheless, and we walked together back to his home.

I never did work out whether his description of me as a dandy meant I looked ridiculous or if it was meant as a back-handed compliment. But the smile never left his face as we walked on. •

What Grandfathers Want

I once wrote a column on Father's Day. Actually, I wrote a bunch over the years. Grandparent's Day or Grandfather's Day is also apparently a thing, but not in our house. Grandfather's Day? How many pairs of socks can one man take?

That said, in the column I pointed out that dads don't need stuff. And grandfathers need even less stuff because they're downsizing and moving into a condo. And all their good stuff went in the garage sale.

So here are a few things your dad really wants for Father's Day. [*And what your grandfather wants too. Every day.*]

Laugh at his jokes. This sounds easy, I know, but think back over the past year. How often did you really laugh at his attempts to be humourous?

Now, I know the jokes weren't funny. Dad's jokes aren't meant to be funny, except to him, which is why after he tells them he begins laughing uncontrollably until, inevitably, he realizes he's the only one laughing.

But did you really need to roll your eyes, groan, shake your head, call him pathetic and ask him to go away if you happened to have friends over? And then did you really have to say to your mother, "Mom, can't you stop him?"

[*Grandfather's Note: Grandchildren never roll their eyes when you tell them jokes. They never call you pathetic. In fact, they usually laugh long and hard. I think this is because kids have more respect and kindness for their grandparents than for their parents. Either that, or they just feel really sorry for you.*]

Listen to one of his stories about when he was young. You've been faking this listening to his stories for a few years now, punctuating your non-listening with "uh-huh" and "wow, really" and "you don't say," but we know you haven't heard a word.

We've seen your eyes glaze over, we've seen you glance repeatedly at the clock on the wall and we have even seen you yawn.

So concentrate and listen hard, just for Father's Day, and then ask a related question that proves you've been paying attention.

Saying, "wow, Dad, you really have lived," doesn't cut it. We can sense sarcasm at a thousand paces.

[*There's not a lot of difference here. But since nobody usually listens to grandparents anyway, give the old man a break . . . even if the story does sound, as it will, highly improbable. Many things improve with age, including tall stories.*]

Ask him to play his favourite record. Records are those things that used to produce music before cassettes, CDs, and iTunes. Listen with him. If he plays "Cat's in the Cradle" by Harry Chapin or, worse, anything by Barry Manilow, you should probably call in professional help.

[*Listen to your grandfather's music, but if he starts to dance, make an excuse and leave the room.*]

Let him win. You know all those years when he lost to you at tennis, when you scored goals past him, when you just beat him in foot races, well, he let you win.

He said he didn't, but he did. It was very difficult for your dad to fake losing. You'd say, "you let me win that point Dad," and he'd say, "no I didn't, I just couldn't handle the speed of that shot."

Think about it. You were four years old. You were also very gullible.

At about the age of, oh, fourteen you started to find that you could beat him more easily at tennis. At twenty or so you could start to beat him at golf. If you'd listened closely you might have heard sobbing.

Your dad isn't gullible, so losing to him and making it look like it's for real is going to be very tough. You might as well work at it now. You'll be a dad one day too.

[*Grandfathers still like to win. But make it something non-physical, like Scrabble or Bananagrams. And when you play, park your brain for a while and slow down. Cough loudly if he nods off.*]

Mow the lawn for him. You should preferably do this while he falls asleep in front of the final round of the US Open. The lawn mower is that thing in the shed that you have to climb over the bicycles to get to. The lawn is that green and brown thing in the backyard covered in weeds and those nice yellow flowers called dandelions.

[*You're lucky. Grandpa's moved into a condo.*]

Teach him how to play a video game. Preferably Tiger Woods Golf or NHL. Be patient. Be gentle. Don't teach him how to play those war games. You'll just scare him.

[*Ditto.*]

Fish out a very old picture of the two or three or four or more of you. Ask him to tell you when and where it was taken. Watch his eyes mist over.

[*Yes. Though he may not remember where it was taken.*]

Make him a sandwich. Fully loaded.

[*Just make it easy to chew.*]

If all else fails, give him that hug. He'll probably smile, maybe crack an embarrassed joke (remember to laugh), but that's all he really wants: Just a tiny piece of you. Little boy blue and the man in the moon. Some things, money won't ever buy. •

You Don't Always Get to Choose ————————

When you first become a grandfather how do you pick what you're called? Gramps, Grandpa, Grandad, Opi? The truth is, I'm afraid, that you don't *always* get to choose.

My Australian brother-in-law is a grandfather, and his grandchildren call him Grumps.

Grumps? Alan doesn't strike me as a grumpy old bastard. Well, sometimes maybe, but that's not a name I'd automatically use to define him.

I ask him if that's an Aussie thing. No, his oldest grandchild started calling him Grumps, and it stuck. He likes it because it's different. Sets him apart from the grandfatherly crowd. The Gramps. You mean the others are all quite affable and warm and loving and you're just a nasty old sod, I suggest.

I leaned towards Grandad because my grandfather was called Grandad. Mayana's other grandfather is called Grandpa, so it avoids confusion. Except my second grandchild, Emma (you'll meet her later), has two grandfathers, both called Grandad. We've given the poor child a lifetime of chaos. Though she has now started calling us "Grandad with a Beard" and "Grandad with a Moustache." Guess we'd better not shave then.

Grandad is not the coolest of titles. It makes me think of a song that was a big novelty number-one hit in the UK in the 1970s. "Grandad" was sung by Clive Dunn, who played the doddery Corporal Jones in *Dad's Army*, a hugely popular TV sitcom about the Home Guard in the Second World War. The song—do find it on YouTube if you must—spent twenty-eight weeks in the hit parade, three weeks at number one, hitting a sentimental nerve.

I was delighted that Mayana at first called me "Grangrad." It always made me smile, but *Grandad*? Maybe I should rethink. The song's reference to the grandad's days being gone stopped me cold. Thanks. No wonder I was reluctant about becoming a grandfather. Find me a rocking chair and a blanket. And nobody had sung a disturbing song about Grangrads. It turns out that many grandchildren mangle their grandparents' names, and they often stick. Hence Grumps instead of Gramps.

My grandfather name is quite traditional and familiar. It's also, according to another brother-in-law, this one an Englishman, more downmarket than Grandpa, which is what he prefers to be called. Only in England could status be attached to your role as a grandparent. Surely he should be called Grandpapa, much more *Downton Abbey*.

There are many variations on the traditional names: Grampa, Grandpappy, Gramps, Grandaddy, Grandpop, Pop, Poppa, Papa, Pops, Pop-pop (*really?*), Bumpy, Boppa and so on. I'm sure, if you're a grandfather, you're incredibly proud of being called Goofball or Golfball or Grungemeister.

According to a couple of pieces I read online, baby-boomer grandfathers, who refuse to leave the 1960s, use names such as G-Daddy or Buddy or G-Pa, to sound somewhat more hip, or artificially hip as the case may be.

Immigrants, or the grandchildren of immigrants, will honour their grandparents by using the title from their countries of origin. I know *Opa*, the German and Dutch familiar form for Grandfather, is popular in North America. I do like the Dutch *Grootvader,* though I doubt very many grandchildren use it in Holland. Unless they're into a Dutch *Star Wars.* "Hey Darth Grootvader."

The Chinese use *YeYe*, the French *Grandpère*, the Spanish *Abuelo*, Italians *Nonno*, Greeks *Papu,* and Russians *Dedushka*, which has a warmth to it. My favourite though is the Hawaiian *Tutu Kane* (pronounced Tootoo Kanay). It sounds respectful and dignified.

As unlike Grandad as you can get. •

2. The Scream

For the first nine months of my grandfatherly relationship with Mayana, I was pretty starstruck with our beautiful little cherubic bundle of joy. Then came the scream—the scream lasted about five hours. Five hours of unmitigated hell. Five hours I'll never get back.

By the end, I felt like I had staggered out of a nightmarish landscape by Edvard Munch.

Mayana was nine months old. And still breastfeeding. It was, appropriately, the day of the Victoria marathon. A day that seemed to go on forever.

Beth and Amy decided to go out kayaking with a local kayaking group for a few hours, and Amy had asked if Jani and I could watch Mayana.

Jani and I said that was fine. We were going to watch the marathon go by anyway. We knew a few people who were running, and we could take Mayana with us. The two of us would be fine looking after her.

The kayakers were due back onshore at three. Jani warned me she could only help me look after Mayana until one because she had to meet some friends for a lunch after the run.

"No prob," I said, confidently. "I'll take her to the beach, and we can play there until her mum kayaks back in. It'll be easy."

[Cue slightly deranged laughter.] Sorry. I still get hysterical when I think back to that afternoon.

The first hour or so was fine. Mayana was somewhat dozy and slept in her stroller while we cheered on the marathoners as they went by us in Oak Bay, the hoity-toity suburb of Victoria. Grandad and aunt were so relaxed, we picked up a couple of cappuccinos at Starbucks and congratulated ourselves on our superior babysitting skills.

Then Mayana, for no apparent reason, began to cry. We jiggled the stroller, whispered reassuring words to her, let her drink a little milk, then let her nibble the corner of a Starbucks cookie, but nothing would mollify her.

Then she began to scream. It was loud. And very scary. We thought a pin was sticking in her, but we checked, and all seemed fine.

The scream got louder.

Marathon runners, passing us by, hesitated briefly, thinking there had been a knife attack on the sidewalk.

It was so loud that spectators the other side of the street began looking across, worryingly.

Then it got louder.

Then louder still.

"We'd better get out of here before we get arrested for child abuse," Jani said.

We wheeled Mayana to a side street, and I got her out of the stroller. I began to comfort her in my arms. The magic touch.

"This'll work," I said. "It always works."

It didn't work. The screams were just as loud, and a lot closer to my ear.

"Here, give her to me," said Jani. "Maybe she'll confuse me for her mom."

It didn't work. Jani at that point had no children and referred to them only as "little aliens." Afterward she told me that that experience with Mayana had been the most effective birth control ever.

"Did I ever scream like that?"

"I'm not sure. I don't think so. But I think parents have the ability to block horrible moments from their memories. I only ever remember you being lovely. Then again, your brother . . . we almost went into counselling."

But as I say, that was afterward, once the trauma had faded. Back to the fateful events of October 13, 2013.

Jani handed Mayana back to me. "I hate to do this, but I have to go. I've organized this big lunch. I hate to leave you like this."

"Don't worry," I said, though by this time I was in a major state of panic. "We'll be fine."

When I hugged Jani goodbye, Mayana managed—against everything that is natural in this world—to scream even more loudly.

We went back to our car, parked just off the main street, and I began to put her in the baby seat.

Now, this is what you *don't* do next. You do *not* speak sharply to a nine-month-old baby.

"That's *enough*," I said. "*Enough. Stop this right now!*"

For a few seconds Mayana stopped screaming, looking at me startled. This person had never done this before . . . he had only ever smiled. Then her face crumpled. She started screaming even more loudly. I closed the door, turned, and saw an older couple glaring at me.

"Ha ha," I said nervously, trying not to look like a heartless beast, and moved swiftly to the driver's door. I wanted to tell the husband and wife that I wasn't like this, that I was a kindly, caring, and gentle grandfather, but I didn't. By now the car was literally shaking with her screams.

I drove to the park with her screams ringing in my ears. I turned up the radio, but the radio was losing, so I turned it off again. I sang "*la la la . . .*" I sang "Baa, Baa, Black Sheep," her favourite. I tried "The Wheels on the Bus," but the cries got worse.

At the park, I decided to change her diaper in the back of the car. Passersby thought I was murdering her. She was only a tad damp.

I looked across at the sea, praying the kayak trip would finish early, but there was nothing on the horizon. I got Mayana out of the car and carried her along the beach. The Scream continued unabated. It was a warm day, and there were plenty of people on the beach, and they all glared as I went past them. They seemed to blame me for all this noise pollution. Not one person offered to help. I still wonder about that. There's this older guy on a beach with a baby who's yelling her head off, and no woman—I'm sorry, I needed a woman, men at this point were beyond useless—came up and offered to help.

Perhaps the maniacal look on my face scared them off.

I tried to comfort Mayana. I felt terrible for her. She needed her mom and was so distraught my heart ached for her. I picked up stones on the beach, pointed at dogs, threw stones in the water, and for a moment she would sniffle and gulp and tear my heart out of my body, and then start screaming again.

And then, finally, I saw boats on the horizon.

"Look," I said. "It's Mommy. Here comes Mommy."

Please, God, let it be Mommy.

The kayaks took an excruciatingly long time to make it to shore. There were about fifteen of them, and Amy was right at the back. I waded into the water with my granddaughter. Up to my waist. Almost up to our necks.

Mayana stopped screaming.

Then she started smiling.

Then she started laughing.

It was a miracle.

A mommy miracle.

"How has she been?" asked my daughter. "Looks like she's hungry for some momma milk."

And suddenly, Mayana was plugged in and feeding happily.

"Have you given poor grandad a hard time?" said Amy.

I was still shaking.

Mayana looked across at me. Reached her hand out to touch mine, and then—unplugging briefly—gave me a big smile.

"I forgive you," I said.

I'm not sure if she forgave me. •

Child of the Century

Mayana is half-Indo-Canadian, half-Caucasian. A mixed-race child.

Her paternal grandparents are, like me and Beth, originally from England, but their families are from India's Punjab. We have become and stayed friends even though their son and our daughter Amy are no longer together.

Mayana is growing up in four households. Her mother's, her father's, and both sets of grandparents'.

She is a modern kid. Pulled between differing cultures and parenting approaches. But she seems incredibly resilient and enjoys the variety that her young life gives her. I guess she knows no different. The nuclear family is a thing of history.

Her mom and dad live in separate homes on Salt Spring Island, a thirty-minute ferry ride from Swartz Bay, north of Victoria. Her other grandparents live in a suburb near Vancouver, and we live in the countryside north of Victoria.

Mayana has toys, books, and clothes in four different places.

She has a sari—and other traditional Indian outfits—in Vancouver that she wears at family weddings and other celebrations. She eats peanut butter on toast with me, and samosas with her Indian grandma. And she eats tofu and beans on Salt Spring, where being alternative is the norm.

A Canadian kid in the twenty-first century. Impossible to pigeonhole. A regular kid. With the most beautiful smile on the planet.

When we were at the park, one day, Mayana asked me to towel off the slide because there were some droplets of water on it, left over from a rainfall earlier in the day.

"It's too wet, Grandad."

"No, it's not . . . just zoom down it."

"No," she said. "Not until it's perfectly dry."

So I used my sweater and dried it off, and made a big, hammy, show of being put out.

"What's your middle name?" I huffed theatrically. "Princess?"

"Yes," she said.

And it is. Kaur is one of her middle names, a mandatory name for baptized female Sikhs. Kaur means "always pure." It also means "princess."

Princess. It figures. I like it. My granddaughter is one of a kind. A princess, indeed. •

3. Fun at the Fair

Every year I take Mayana to a fall fair. I started when she was less than a year old, pushing her around in her stroller to see the animals and the rides and the sights and sounds of multicoloured midway mayhem.

That first year was the PNE (Pacific National Exhibition), the biggest fair in Western Canada. She fell asleep during the horse show, and when she awoke, I pledged to her that I would take her to a fall fair every year. Then she cried when I took her on a ride in which cars moved around a circular track at a snail's pace.

Even so, the tradition had begun.

The second year we went, she stayed awake during the horse show, had her first taste of cotton candy ("Don't tell your mother!"), and went on a giant slide. That last slide thing didn't work out so well.

The giant slide wasn't that big, but to a kid under the age of two, I suppose it looked pretty intimidating. I talked her into it.

"Look, we walk to the top, I sit on that mat and then you sit on my lap, and I'll hold you really close and we'll slide to the bottom," I said. "Look at the kids at the bottom, they're all smiling. They all had fun."

Mayana didn't seem convinced. Perhaps the screams of those sliding down the giant slide influenced her. But after about three minutes she said okay.

We climbed to the top of the slide, hand-in-hand. It took a few moments to get the mat sorted when Mayana, who had by this time had a good look around, and a long look down, had come to a decision.

"No, Grandad. I don't want to go."

There were about ten kids lined up behind us on the steps, all significantly older than Mayana.

"It'll be fine," I said, adding somewhat pathetically, "Grandad wouldn't do anything to hurt you, would he?" Resorting to the third person is always a suspect approach. But she fell for it.

"Okay."

So we went down the slide. Now, I must confess I had no idea it would go that fast. We zoomed down the slide at breakneck speed. Neither of us spoke or screamed. Perhaps we were in shock.

We reached the end of the slide. Mayana stood up and put her hands on her hips in indignation. I wondered where she'd learned that pose.

"Grandad, that was SCARY," she said in capital letters. Then she began to cry.

I picked her up and held her close. "I'm sorry, sweetheart. I guess that was faster than we expected. Now, would you like to go on the roller coaster?" I was joking. Grandfathers are allowed to say stupid things like that.

The cotton candy was the inevitable next move. It worked very well. Then we went off to pat some pigs and sheep in the animal barns.

When she was two years old, I took her to a smaller fall fair near our home close to Victoria. By this time, she wanted to go on a few kiddie rides, go fishing for prizes at the sideshows, and pat the Shetland ponies in the barns. She had an ice cream and a cotton candy on the same day, something she pronounced super-awesome.

I look forward to going to the fair with Mayana. It's our thing. Towards the end of the summer when she was three, we went to the smaller fair again. We went on a few rides, patted some animals, clucked at the chickens, and laughed at the ice-cream-eating contest.

And the best thing. They had a giant slide.

"Want to go on it?" I asked her.

"Sure," she said. This one was twice as high as the one that scared us to bits a couple of years earlier. Small kids have short memories.

This slide had a huge lineup. But we stood there for a few minutes when I realized there would be a height limit. They had one of those YOU MUST BE THIS TALL TO RIDE cut-outs at the entrance, so I asked a mom to hold my place while Mayana and I went to the front of the line to see if she'd make the height.

She did. By a centimetre. I went back in line. We waited another five minutes and were close to the front when Mayana said, "I need to go to the washroom."

"Now? Right this second?"

"Yes," and she started joggling up and down. "Right now."

I asked the mom to hold my place again, picked up Mayana, and we went careening around the fun fair. Finally, we found washrooms in the arts and crafts building. There was a lineup at the women's washroom. The men's was empty.

I took her in, put her in one of the stalls, closed the door, stood on guard. "Now hurry or we'll have to wait ages to get on the slide again."

After about thirty seconds a father came in with his young son and started washing his face, which was covered with cotton candy. We were losing valuable seconds.

"Mayana," I said theatrically, also because I felt I looked a little weird hanging around inside a washroom, "are you done yet?"

"No yet?"

"What's taking so long."

"I needed a poo."

The father looked across at me and smiled. "Congratulations," he said. "You win first prize."

A minute or so later, we zoomed back to the giant slide, and there was the mom and her son. I was exhausted, but we'd made it. "Thank you," I said.

"No problem," said the mom. "I wonder if you could do me a favour. My son's not big enough to go up on his own. Could you take him."

Which is why I struggled to the top of the giant mega slide with two preschoolers, put them both on sacks alongside me, struggled somewhat stiffly onto my own sack, and then slid at something like a thousand miles an hour down a slide that took my breath and most of my stomach away.

We got to the bottom. I was drained.

Mayana was standing. "That was fun, Grandad. Can we do it again?"

We did.

Next year, she says she wants us to go on the roller coaster. I don't think she's joking. •

I Won't

It is understood that grandchildren are wondrous little beings with cherubic faces and Nobel prize-winning intelligence, and the creative skills of a Picasso or Pisarro.

But there's the other side. The dark side.

"Finish your dinner, sweetheart."

"No."

"Come on, just one bite."

"No. Don't want to."

And these are the teenagers. Okay, kidding. But small children do have a facility to use one word, quite often.

"Won't."

Won't eat that pasta, *won't* come down to the beach, *won't* pick up that toy, *won't* tidy up that sock, *won't* put on that boot, *won't* hold Grandad's hand, *won't* do up that button.

They're testing us, of course. Seeing how long they can push our buttons.

My wife handles all this well. No such word as "won't," she says, and tells them to get on with it and they do. Grandmothers have this facility to engender instant respect and obedience. They cajole, encourage, look stern while still having lovely smiles on their faces, and the kids and grandkids do what they're told.

Grandfathers? Well, mostly, we're useless at getting any small child to do what we want them to do if they're not in the mood. We don't want to get angry with them, so we try other techniques. Bribery. Or being sad—which is, in and of itself, really sad.

Here's how it works. Let's say there are two carrots, a piece of lettuce, some macaroni and cheese, and a slice of bread on the plate. Your grandchild stops eating and refuses to eat any more.

Here's how a grandmother does it.

"Okay, let's see you eat that up. You don't have to eat all of it. But I want to see you trying. Let's try this carrot. Okay."

Okay is not a question. It's a statement. Now, this doesn't

always work, but often it does, and within a few seconds the child is munching on a carrot, then reaches for a piece of lettuce, and then is eating up the mac and cheese.

The grandfather has a different approach.

"Eat that up, please."

Nothing.

"Come on. Did you hear me? I want this all eaten up."

Silence.

"Come on. You're not going to leave the table until you've eaten every bit."

Louder silence.

"Did you hear me? Eat it up. Come on, I'll let you have some ice cream if you eat that carrot. And some candy. And you can watch *The Wiggles*. And I'll read you three stories. Look, let me make this spoon of mac and cheese into a plane and fly it into your mouth."

And then, slowly, they nibble at the edge of a carrot.

"Can I have my ice cream now, Grandad?"

See, not so bad. We got there in the end. •

Food, Glorious Food

When we were kids, we ate mac and cheese, wieners, pizza, egg sandwiches (on white bread, naturally), fish fingers, and any meat or cheese or other foodstuff that had been thoroughly processed.

Mayana loves avocado. And papaya. And smoked salmon. Three things I'd never heard of when I was her age. Her mom doesn't like her to eat too much bread or sugar because she thinks it might affect her brain. I try not to take that as a personal insult.

The food available in the modern world is stunning. Whatever we want to eat from anywhere on the planet is available. Dragon fruit? Easy. Moroccan spices? No problem. Did you know what sushi was when you were three years old? Unlikely. My grandkids love sushi. And quesadillas. At their age I couldn't pronounce quesadillas.

We who grew up after the Second World War in England, in particular, were pretty much starved of exotic foodstuff. Rationing was over, but there weren't any supermarkets, and many of us lived hand-to-mouth.

My father loved to eat *bread and dripping*. Even today I find that stunning, in an artery-clogging kind of way. White bread smeared with the fat, or drippings, left over in the pan from the Sunday roast— pork or lamb or beef fat. Then he would liberally cover it with plenty of salt. My dad lived until the age of ninety. So it didn't seem to do him much harm.

Vegetarians were essentially invisible. I'm sure they were around, but I never saw them. My wife and daughters are vegetarian and have been for a while (I am a more recent convert), and though Mayana eats fish, she sure eats a lot more vegetables than I did when I was her age. Then again, in my defence, vegetables in England in the fifties were almost inedible. Mothers (as fathers rarely cooked) boiled the vegetables for so long it was almost impossible to tell what you were eating. Much of it tasted like a green sludge, especially the cabbage. Raw veggies? Mayana eats them all the time for snacks, but I can't honestly remember ever eating vegetables uncooked. Just overcooked.

But there are similarities. Mayana loves me to make her a boiled egg with little soldiers—cut-up pieces of toast—on the side for dipping into the runny yolk. I used to love those too. Still do, in fact.

Cereal or porridge are also breakfast staples, as they were back then, and we prefer anything that has chocolate or sugar in the title.

Mayana gets plenty of fresh fruit. When I was a kid, we'd get tinned pineapple chunks or peaches with Carnation cream.

I also got plenty of home baking. My mother made meat and potato pies, apple pies, blackberry crumbles, rice puddings, bread and butter puddings, often accompanied by thick, yellow Bird's Custard. We'd have English trifles, full of jelly and custard and leftover cake.

The biggest treat my mother gave us as a snack was a chocolate sandwich. Fry's sold a wafer-thin bar of chocolate that she'd place between white bread and butter. It was unbelievably decadent and, even then, very wrong on all kinds of nutritional levels. We also had chocolate spread, an English version of Nutella. English children always had bad teeth.

I asked Mayana what she'd like for lunch the other day.

"Guacamole, please, Grandad," she said. "With a few corn chips. And a little salsa, but not too, too hot."

We've come a long way from bread and dripping and Spam, that pink, processed kind of indeterminate meat, a cheaper ham, which was a staple of my childhood. It's big in Hawaii too—where American soldiers ate it during the Second World War—and is still sold in supermarkets and served in restaurants. Go figure.

When I was a kid, I loved to don an apron and bake with my mum. She'd give me some leftover pastry to make jam tarts or lemon-curd tarts.

Mayana loves that too. We make cinnamon buns and pancakes and crepes, and the other week we made some banana bread. She declared it "dohlicious."

The kitchen is always a disaster afterwards, with flour and eggshells and dollops of this or that covering the counters.

"Here," I'll say, channelling my own mother, "take this piece of pastry, fill it with jam and roll it up, and it can be your special jam roly-poly."

She laughs at the word.

"You're roly-poly, Grandad. Did they name this after you?"

A friend of mine has a bumper sticker he's quite proud of: I LOVE ANIMALS. I COULD EAT THEM ALL DAY.

That still tickles my funny bone even if, at the time of writing, I haven't eaten meat for two years. Okay, I still eat seafood, so I'm not a full-blown veggie; I'm what they call a pescatarian.

I stopped eating meat around Christmas 2017. I'd started to see the animals, rather than the cuts of meat. I didn't eat rabbit because I'd read *Watership Down* or venison because of *Bambi*. I liked my meat heavily disguised, preferably as hamburger or sausages, though I made an exception with rack of lamb, which still makes my mouth water when I write those words on the page. Rack of lamb—so I won't be mentioning that again. Or prime rib. Or, disturbingly, Kentucky Fried Chicken, which was one of my guiltiest pleasures, even when the fat was dripping down my chin and my digits were finger-licking bad.

I went cold turkey. I guess that should be cold tofu. And turkey was to blame. While some have this Norman Rockwell image of a family huddled around a plump turkey at the Christmas table, all I began to see was an unfortunate animal on its back with its head chopped off and its legs stuck in the air. And I never did rhapsodize about sticking my hand up its butt and stuffing it with breadcrumbs and chestnuts.

But, yes, for most of my life, I enjoyed the taste and the cooking of it for Christmas. I even enjoyed eating cold turkey and cranberry sandwiches for a week after Christmas Day.

When I made my announcement, my sons didn't believe I'd hang in for long. That February the three of us went on a golf/baseball/hockey trip to Arizona, and they were convinced I'd crack at the first menu that had ribs on it. But I held on, to their amazement.

There was an unfortunate moment when we went into an In-N-Out Burger after hiking up and down a mountain. The boys ordered a burger and fries, and I asked the server if they had a vegetarian option.

"Absolutely, sir. Where are you sitting? I'll bring it over to you."

The boys picked up their plump burgers and fries and started munching happily away.

Then my order arrived. I opened the bun to look inside. There was nothing there. Except a pale piece of lettuce and a slice of tomato. No burger. Nothing. We all started laughing.

"Wanna quick bite of mine?" offered Tim. "We won't tell anybody."

I ate my sad bun anyway. With a Diet Coke and a few French fries.

I'm sure that by now In-N-Out Burger has a more interesting veggie options, since vegetarianism is becoming more mainstream. Whenever I mention to people that I don't eat meat they have two responses.

"Do you feel healthier?"

Nope. Can't say I do.

Or: "You don't say. I'm eating much less meat than I used to." And (if it's a couple) "Aren't we, Darling? We probably only eat meat twice a week. Or even less."

I'm not judgmental, or like some kind of reformed smoker, a non-meat-eating evangelist. It's just something I choose to do. And life has become a whole lot easier now that Beyond Meat burgers have come into my life to sate my occasional meat craving.

I also don't do smug. Well, I try not to. Going veggie isn't for everyone.

Which brings us to Mayana. My eldest granddaughter went vegetarian a few months ago, at the age of nine.

"Do you think that's okay?" I asked my wife. "I mean, she's awfully young."

My wife reminded me that we were a tad worried when our daughters went veggie when they were ten and twelve, respectively. Which meant all the females in the family were non-meat eaters while the three males, including me at the time, were dedicated carnivores. Yes, we were a stereotype. The girls were intelligent, caring, modern. The males were grunting cavemen.

My wife explained that as long as the girls had a rounded diet, they'd be fine. There was, she said, too much of a focus on protein, and that you got plenty of it from other sources. We had plenty of cheese, beans, eggs, oats, and, obviously, fish.

Mayana is fit and healthy and bouncing around like Tigger and seems to be thriving on her non-meat diet. And as there are more and more interesting veggie sources of protein and other nutritionally necessary foods available, being a non-meat eater is not going to set off any alarms.

Emma and Linden aren't vegetarian, nor is their father. This past Christmas, he decided to cook a prime rib roast for Christmas dinner. But because he doesn't eat a lot of meat, he repeatedly asked me questions about how to cook it.

I gave him advice before, during, and after the cooking process, and it turned out fine. It smelled wonderful. Better than the veggie alternative, a nut roast. But veggies and carnivores broke bread together happily. And we will for some time.

Until meat eating is made illegal, that is. Ha! Wanna try my deep-fried tofu? It's to die for. •

4. My Summer with Mayana

[Part One]

The summer of 2013 was something of a turning point for me as a grandad—for a couple of reasons. First, Amy was taking an intense yoga instructor's course, and I had the opportunity to step up and watch Mayana. This meant covering for Amy three or four days a week during class time for the *entire* summer. This would be some heavy-duty grandadding. What could be better than that? I would often be staying up on Salt Spring Island with them to cut down on the travel both for me and Mayana. I was excited. And if that weren't enough to make a grandad smile, my younger daughter, Jani, was also expecting. (I guess the birth control effect of the "screaming incident" had worn off by then.) I figured my grandad cred would be at an all-time high by the time grandchild number two made an appearance sometime in July.

Mayana too was excited, and we both went into that summer with high spirits. I was now *Grandad* rather than *Grangrad*, having grangraduated to a more conventional position.

During my summer with Mayana, I was going to teach her a lot of things.

How to ride a bike.

How to sing "Yellow Submarine."

How to say please and thank you and all that stuff we grownups find kind of important.

How to write her name.

How to have fun.

Instead, I think I learned more from her than she learned from me. Mostly, how to slow down and not only smell the roses—but count them. And count them again. And again. And again.

How many red ones? And blue ones? And white ones? And do we prefer the white ones, or are the red ones prettier?

I also learned, for instance, that washing your car can be a far more memorable experience if you let your three-and-a-half-year-old granddaughter hold the hose. The car didn't get very wet, but we did.

That summer would also prove a pivotal and somewhat emotional time for me for another reason. After more than forty-five years of working as a journalist, I was leaving the daily grind of journalism and heading to the dreaded r-word: retirement.

Some guys yearn for retirement. I had mixed feelings. Retirement meant all the clichés to me . . . a lack of purpose, doddering into a life of seniors' specials and matinée movies, a world of baggy cardigans and pinochle or euchre, whatever they are. Someone told me I was old enough now to play pickleball, a kind of tennis for old people. I could still play tennis, thank you very much—could still serve the occasional ace—and here I was already consigned to the shuffleboard of life.

In truth, I'm not sure how the idea of me looking after Mayana came up. I might have volunteered. Or, more likely, someone volunteered me. Amy was a single mother by then, so it would be tricky to have Mayana cared for. And besides, it was patently obvious that everyone else was busy, and I had nothing useful to do. Beth was kayak guiding on Quadra Island for the summer, cavorting with orcas and dolphins and sea stars and such. And San, Mayana's father, was travelling.

I don't want you to get the idea that I had no idea what to do when it came to looking after small children.

I'd always been an okay dad. Well, my four kids still hang out with me, so that's good, right? We get on well. We get together a lot, particularly when I pay for dinner.

I went to all their soccer and hockey games, even coached them all for a time. I once spent two days watching my eldest daughter compete in a synchronized swimming competition (greater love hath no parent), and we all went on camping trips and bike trips and on plenty of vacations together, and we played a lot and laughed a lot. Some called us the Partridge Family—though I don't think they all meant it kindly.

To paraphrase Mark Twain, when my kids were teenagers, they found me so ignorant they could barely stand being with me. But by the time they'd reached their twenties they were astonished at how much the old man had learned in just a few years.

But that was then. This grandfather stuff was different.

While my kids were growing up, being a dad was a juggling act. I did pretty time-intensive jobs. I was editor-in-chief of two of Canada's biggest newspapers, the *Vancouver Province* and then the *Vancouver Sun*, and news director of one of the country's bigger TV stations, BCTV News (which became Global). For a couple of years, I was West Coast correspondent for the country's largest newspaper chain, Southam News, which meant I was on the road a lot. I flitted between work and home, and—thanks mostly to Beth, who was supermom incarnate—raising four kids went well.

But this nearly full-time grandfather thing—this was something new. My wife, now nailing grandmother, or Nani, as she likes to be called, wasn't around to help.

Most grandmothers seem to be naturals at this grandmothering thing. For grandpas, it doesn't always come naturally. Babies are foreign beings, devoid of anything you can hold onto with any degree of confidence. They cry, they sleep, they eat. And don't do much more.

As soon as Mayana was born, Beth knew what to do. She cuddled her close, cooed in her ear, brushed her hair with loving hands, sang her gentle songs, rocked her to sleep.

She knew how to comfort her.

As Mayana grew older, Beth had a special bond with her. I thought I was pretty close to my granddaughter, but Beth knew instinctively how to be with her.

And it's always been that way. Grandmothers seem to have this capacity for endless patience. They'll play silly games on the floor, or paint pictures, or do puzzles, or sing nursery rhymes for hours, while I'm already showing signs of fatigue.

Grandfathers typically join in when the grandchild is about three years old, somewhere after toilet training and before kindergarten.

We're good with balls—soccer balls, tennis balls, baseballs, footballs—but we are not naturals at grandfathering.

I think men are getting better than they ever did at parenting. My generation started to get into it big time, but my daughters' generation is amazing. The dads do more cooking and washing and cleaning and parenting than any of their forbears. With most moms working full time, that's as it should be. It's a shared experience. And this is the twenty-first century.

But grandparenting? Our role models are now gone, so we kind of make it up as we go along.

So, for much of the summer, it was just me and Mayana.

I didn't get it all right. But we both survived. And she still talks to me too. And gives me big hugs. •

A Slow Walk with Mayana

It started with a slow walk. The first day of the summer that I looked after Mayana began with what I expected would be a quick stroll to a small playground. It would normally take me five minutes at most to walk there.

This day it took us almost an hour.

We stopped to look at flowers. Then bees. Then butterflies. Then we blew dandelions. We picked buttercups. And looked at horses in a field. Then we patted a dog. And talked to the owner. And then we talked to the dog.

Mayana, on this first day of the rest of my life, taught me on our first full morning together to slow down. Not just slow down. But also come to a full stop. And sometimes, go backwards.

Until that week I had been running a turbulent, crazy TV newsroom in Vancouver. My life was organized chaos, particularly on days of big breaking news, when nobody had time to blink, let alone think.

One of my last jobs was to oversee our coverage of an election. I'd commissioned polling, argued with party officials about the format of the TV debates, pushed for us to get to the heart of the issues, gone through graphics and results systems and online coverage—and now here I was staring at a crack in the road.

"Why is the road broken?"

"It's not broken, it's just cracked a bit."

"Will we fall in?"

"Well, no, it's just a small crack."

"Will it get bigger and bigger and then we'll fall in?"

"I don't think so."

Stopping to smell the roses as a hard-nosed newsman was out of the question. Today, I wasn't only smelling them—in the neighbours' front yards—I was also counting them, testing Mayana on the various colours (her favourite is purple) and spotting as many bees as we could.

"They won't hurt us, grandad. The bees are friendly if you don't hurt them." She'd learned that much.

"Do you know why they're buzzing around the flowers?" I asked.

She didn't, and frankly, I didn't know much more since I was never a gardener nor paid much attention in biology classes, but I kind of stumbled through a hazy description of what bees do with pollen and how they make honey and also that, in this particular society, the Queen Bee rules. Kind of like at our house, I said.

You'd have thought running newsrooms—newspaper and broadcast—would have been perfect training for looking after a grandchild. I always likened my job to that of a kindergarten teacher. There were certainly tantrums and tears. And bruised egos rather than bruised knees.

I joked, when I was in the news world, that I learned more from Robert Fulghum than all the management courses I went on over the years. Fulghum wrote the delightful book *All I Really Know I Learned in Kindergarten*. An essayist and former Unitarian minister, Fulghum wrote his huge bestseller in 1986. It should be republished for a new generation.

Some of the advice?

Share everything.

Don't hit people.

Live a balanced life.

Learn some and think some.

Hold hands and stick together.

Be aware of wonder.

"Grandad, what's that pink flower called?"

I had absolutely no idea.

"A geranium," I said. "Or a chrysanthemum, maybe?"

"A chriscinnamon?"

"Something like that. Or maybe a daisy."

We counted more than fifty butterflies on our walk, most of them white, a couple of them more colourful. We watched them land on the flowers and then flutter off in search of more adventure. I honestly hadn't realized there were so many butterflies on our street. I guess I had failed to look properly. My head was usually full of other stuff.

Mayana decided she'd rather be a butterfly than a bee. She didn't want people to be scared of her.

"Everyone loves butterflies. And they can fly so high. Look, Grandad. That one's higher than that big tree." Then she held my hand. "What do you want to be, Grandad?"

It was a good question. Until that moment I'd been somewhat confused about who I was after leaving the newsroom. It defined me. I loved being in the middle of all the noise, in the middle of a vital, relevant world, and I was trying to come to terms with what and who I now was. I never really wanted to be "retired" and snapped at anyone who even suggested I was now in retirement.

But right then, right at that very moment, while the world slowed to a perfect stop, while my granddaughter clung onto my hand and looked up at me with large, brown innocent eyes, I knew one of the things that I wanted to be.

A grandfather might be a cool thing after all. •

Underducks

The playground is magical. And a minefield—albeit a magical minefield. We spent a lot of time in playgrounds that summer.

There was stuff to climb on—and fall off of. There were slides to slide down, but some way too slippery and way too fast. There were swings to swing on, but I told Mayana to hold on for dear life and warned her not to get too dizzy on those roundabouts.

One of the things you realize as you get older is that you have a lower threshold for swings and roundabouts than when you were three years old. I am still reeling after going on Disneyland's Space Mountain three times in a row when my own kids were younger.

I'd happily lift Mayana onto the climbing frames. But then she'd get stuck at the top. Beyond my reach.

"Come and jump into my arms."

"It's too far, Grandad."

"No, it isn't."

But it *was*, so I'd climb up tiny steps or pull myself up onto dangling chains and ropes, and rescue her, and then the two of us would clamber down together.

"Why are you holding your back, Grandad?"

"Nothing, just a slight twinge is all."

Backache, I discovered that summer, is one of the hazards of being a grandparent. Your grandchild wants to be carried, lifted, pushed, and pulled. I could do it a lot more efficiently when I was a father. A grandfather life hack: Always carry ibuprofen with you on an outing with the grandkids.

In the playground, your grandkids want you to go the other end of the teeter-totter. Or, more dangerously, give them an underduck.

"Underduck, Grandad. Underduck!"

If you don't know what an underduck is, you haven't spent enough time playing with your kids. You push the swing right above your head, then run forward and under the swing before it returns at high speed.

There are three things to know about underducks for smaller children:

First, don't push too hard, or you'll send them into orbit.

Second, push hard enough, or the swing will come back and hit you on your head.

Third, there's no such thing as only one underduck. Like everything else with your grandchild, it has to be repeated until you're bored out of your mind or your back goes into spasms. •

I Wanna Hold Your Hand

There was this moment, as magical as any I can think of, a few days into our summer together when my granddaughter's tiny hand snaked gently into mine. We were walking towards a park, an unfamiliar park, and this small gesture signified . . . what? Reassurance? Belonging? I found it comforting. Us against the world. This wasn't me reaching out for *her* hand as we crossed a busy street, but Mayana needing *my* hand for help. I was her safety. I loved it.

Holding hands. It sounds simple, but it's one of life's wonders. It's one of the things I love most.

As adults we remember holding hands with the ones we love or loved. That first girlfriend, when our hands clasped, and our palms were sweaty and probably shaking too.

Wives and husbands. Holding hands in public. That sense of belonging, of partnership, of togetherness. We touch . . . our fingers touch.

Even in old age, with arthritic fingers and liver spots on the backs of our hands, we feel a thrill when we hold hands with the ones we love. Some older people don't hold hands anymore. I find that very sad.

I don't hold hands with my kids anymore. I'm not sure when it stopped. Probably when they were young teenagers and embarrassed by any parental signs of affection, particularly in front of their friends. My sons and daughters still hug me and my wife when we meet, and a few weeks ago my youngest daughter walked arm-in-arm with me down the street, but hand-holding with your kids is a thing of yesteryear.

Which is why holding hands with your grandchild feels so very special. Briefly, too briefly, you can hang on literally and figuratively to the past. By your fingertips. I guess that's why your grandchildren are important—they help you remember all those small things you did with your own kids. You never wanted your kids to grow up. Or you wanted a moment frozen in time, like that summer holiday at the beach with endless sun and so much laughter. And here, now, with a grandchild, you get to feel it all over again. Grandchildren are second chances.

Usually, I'm the instigator of hand-holding. "Here, hold my hand as we cross the street." Or "Stay close to me, Mayana. Come and hold my hand." And she does.

But when she does it of her own accord, when she searches for my hand and grabs it, then it becomes something even more significant.

"Here, Grandad, come and see this," she will say, and hold my hand and lead me to the swing or to a shop window or to see a bee buzzing on a flower.

Sometimes she will hold my hand when she's scared. Maybe of the dark, perhaps because we're about to meet another adult and she's uncertain or intimidated.

Sometimes, and this is my favourite moment of all, her hand just snakes into mine for no reason.

Well, no reason except I'm her grandad, and I'm her protector, old friend, confidant, playmate, singing buddy, joke-teller and all-round fun person.

And, maybe, just maybe because she feels me squeeze her hand just a little tightly whenever she puts it there. •

Take Me for a Ride

We didn't just walk or go to the park when we went outside. We drove a lot too. Me in front, Mayana in the back in her child's seat. A child's seat is the most godawful contraption in the world. The straps are too loose, or the buckle won't do up, or you can't find where the seatbelt clicks in. You're exhausted when you finally sit in your own seat.

Driving with Mayana is never boring. Usually, when I drive alone, I go into a dull overdrive, not really paying attention to much around me, occasionally listening to the radio. Letting my mind wander. Yet still paying attention to the road.

When you have a three-year-old granddaughter in the kid's chair in the back, you look at her through the rear-view mirror almost as much as the road ahead. But you drive extra carefully. I hate those BABY ON BOARD stickers on the rear of cars, but I drive like I have one that says DON'T EVEN THINK OF COMING CLOSE TO ANYONE IN THE BACK OF THIS VEHICLE. Mayana sometimes complains I drive too slowly. With her, I can't help it.

We sing a lot in the car. Everything from "Baa, Baa, Black Sheep" to "The Wheels on the Bus" to a whole panoply of Raffi songs. I used to sing Raffi songs to my kids when they were small, and now I get a kick out of singing "Baby Beluga" and "Shake Your Sillies Out" and our favourite, "It's Mine but You Can Have Some." That one works on all kinds of levels, particularly when I want to snag some of her candy.

I got really happy when I taught her "Yellow Submarine." I didn't mind singing it again and again while she learned it. I did get irked a few months later, however, when, in the back of the car . . .

"Listen to this song, Grandad. My dad taught it to me." She started singing.

"That's 'Yellow Submarine'! *I* taught you that song," I said, somewhat wounded.

"No, my dad did," she insisted.

I decided to back off gracefully. "Then he did, about three months after I did," I said under my breath.

46

Sometimes we do quizzes in the car, like I used to do with my own kids when they were young.

Easy ones. "What does a cow say?" Trickier ones. "What does a hyena say?" Funny ones. "What does a kid eating mud say?"

A: "Yeeeeeuch."

Sometimes we just talk. She asks me stuff, easy stuff like where are we going, when are we getting there, where's Nani, where's Uncle Tim, why are you driving so slowly, Grandad?

One day she said, "I figured something out, Grandad. Adults talk. Kids play."

"Yes," I said, "sometimes we talk and talk and talk." "Yes," said Mayana. "You should play more. It's more fun."

A therapy session from my granddaughter. Play more. Talk less. Not a bad mantra.

Once, after we'd been swimming—which turned out to be one of Mayana's favourite things to do—we decided we'd head to a kids' movie playing at the nearby Cineplex. I was chatting and singing and then I looked in the rear-view mirror and noticed that her eyelids were drooping.

"Do you want to see the movie? Or shall we leave it another day?"

"Another day, Grandad," she said, and was instantly asleep.

And that is one of the loveliest things you'll ever see in your rear-view mirror. •

5. Getting the Call

One morning that summer, I got a phone call.

"Baby's coming," said my son-in-law, Chris, Jani's husband.

I was just getting out of bed on a beautiful July morning on Salt Spring Island, where I had been staying with Amy and Mayana. I had been groggy when I answered the phone. Suddenly I was wide awake and jolted into action.

I woke up my daughter and granddaughter. "I have to rush," I said. And then, to Mayana: "Looks like you're about to have a cousin."

She started clapping.

Amy didn't have classes that day and promised to come over later in the afternoon, once the baby was born.

"Me too," said Mayana, full of excitement.

I called my wife. "On my way," she said.

We were both, coincidentally, on small islands. Me on Salt Spring, two hours away, and my wife on Quadra Island, nearer five hours.

We got there the same time.

"I drove like the wind," she said.

We walked into the hospital together. "Grandad," she said, "we are going to have our second grandchild today." We hugged.

I spent most of that day in a waiting room in the maternity wing. My wife and Chris were in the birthing room with Jani. She didn't want me in there.

"That's okay," I said. "I get it."

I was given regular updates. As were two other grandfathers in the room. This, I guess, is what it felt like for expectant fathers before dads became part of the birth process. I saw all four of my kids born, two of them at home, and from a man's point of view anyway, those births were a lot easier. Because I knew what was going on.

Every now and then we'd hear a scream, a blood-curdling yell, from one of the birthing rooms, and we three grandfathers would look at each other with fear in our eyes. Our daughters were in there. Our little girls. Going through hell.

At one point, about nine hours after we got in there, I heard Jani yowl.

"Nooooooo . . ."

It was her voice, all right. Unmistakeable. So loud, so distraught, so sickeningly sorrowful, that we thought something terrible must have happened. I had to stop myself from rushing into the room. I waited five minutes before my wife appeared.

"All good," she said. "Just taking a long time."

All good? How could that wail be good, in any way at all? But I relaxed some.

"When is it coming?" I asked, one of the all-time stupid questions. My priceless senior's moment.

"When it's ready," she said. "Jani's hanging in there. She's amazing."

The other grandfathers got their calls. One granddaughter. One grandson.

I was sent to get flowers and a card. Two cards. One for a boy, one for a girl. I got two different balloons too.

Emma, lovely Emma, my beautiful second granddaughter, was born late in the day on July 5. I first saw her in my daughter's arms. Jani looked like she'd been run over by an express train, but still smiled.

"You look beautiful," I said. "And so does she." And I kissed them both.

And they did. Men don't usually *get* babies. Not as much as women do. Women immediately oooh and aaaah and become Jell-O around newborns. Men *get* the miracle of it all, but they're confronted with a nearly bald, squished-up miniature version of Winston Churchill.

Emma didn't look like that. Not to me. She was magical and miraculous from the moment she was born. When you're a father or a grandfather, you see things other guys don't see.

You always will.

Later, when Amy and Mayana arrived to greet Emma, there was a perfect union of four young ladies. Our two daughters with their daughters.

Mayana was over the moon with excitement, and held Emma in her arms for a while, smiling the entire time. They have been great buddies ever since.

Mayana has always treated Emma as her kid sister, beaming whenever she sees her. For a long time (once she learned how to talk), Emma simply called Mayana *cousin*, as in, "Hey, cousin, what shall we do today?" "Cousin, shall we play in my room?"

But that day, Emma was a magical baby. And there was plenty of magic still to come. •

Babysitting Emma

One afternoon I babysat Emma at her home. She was about six months old, and I had a free afternoon and was available and nobody else could do it.

"She's asleep and she'll probably stay asleep until Chris gets home," said Jani reassuringly, so I sat at the dining table with a book, relaxed.

And then all hell broke loose.

Jani had been gone less than two minutes before the screaming started. You will remember I had a screaming incident with Mayana. You'd be forgiven for thinking that perhaps that little episode would have prepared me for this. It did not.

I rushed into Emma's bedroom, checked she wasn't being impaled by a safety pin, checked her diaper (fine), checked every other part of her body that might be pinched, squeezed, or damaged, established she seemed in full working order, and then hugged her close. That comforted her for, oh, about five seconds.

I jiggled her and walked her around and looked at the clock. It would be at least three hours before Chris would come home. So I had to get her back to sleep.

I didn't.

For the next three hours I sang to her—I even pulled out a guitar to try and make it more entertaining. I played with toys for her, did little shows with stuffies, walked her around the room. Fed her. None of it worked.

She alternated between screaming and sobbing. Sobbing! That was almost worse. When you see your helpless six-month-old grand-daughter sobbing, it breaks your heart. You want to protect her, not produce sobs.

I remembered, too vividly, almost thirty years earlier when I had gotten up in the middle of the night when Jani was crying. We lived in Ottawa then, and she was the same age as Emma was now. I told my wife I'd take a middle-of-the-night shift. Jani wouldn't stop crying either. At one point, to my eternal shame, I got angry with my six-month-old daughter.

"That's *enough!*" I shouted, looking straight into her eyes.

She looked confused, scared, and then she started sobbing. It is a moment I will never forget.

And I remembered it now—and my similar lapse with Mayana when she was only a little older than Emma. I would not get angry with this tiny child who was depending on me. So I sang some more. Well, sang my whole repertoire if truth be told. I walked her up and down the living room, comforted her, sometimes tried to put her back in her crib—at which point she would scream loudly enough to wake the dead—and after two hours and forty-five minutes decided I would take her to the tiny children's playground at the rear of the apartment complex.

Which is where my son-in-law found me, swinging on a swing with Emma in my arms where she had, *mercifully*, fallen asleep.

"Wow," said Chris. "You look like you've been run over by a truck."

"No, we're just fine," I lied.

"Well," he said. "*She* looks fine anyway. *You* look like you need serious medical attention." •

Squeals

It's not all pussy willows and cattails when you spend time with a tiny granddaughter. Sometimes—usually when you have a monumental headache and all you need is peace and quiet and a darkened room in which to die—there's the squealing.

Little girls take squealing to a whole new annoying decibel level. Somewhere up there with twenty-five Italian motor scooters roaring past you like a swarm of angry mosquitoes, or Barry Manilow singing "I Write the Songs."

I'm sure little boys squeal too. They're certainly loud. But little girls, when they get together, sound like mice about to have their tails cut off with a carving knife. They run around the house, bouncing off sofas (well, the sofa in which I'm sitting) and punctuate every third step with a piercing scream.

Now, it must be said that parents—today's parents who appear to indulge every excess of their tiny offspring (did I really just write that?)—seem oblivious to the screams. Two sets of parents will sit together discussing, usually, the high cost of childcare (forgetting grandparents are doing it for free) or comparing notes on the latest new spa or four-star restaurant, while their children run around them, bouncing off the ceiling, screaming for their lives. There could be an axe murderer on the loose, for Pete's sake, but the parents would be oblivious to anything outside their own conversation.

Actually, maybe that's something they *have* to do: tune out their children's screams so they can go on acting like real human beings. It's a defence mechanism. Otherwise they'd never get to talk to another grownup.

Maybe grandparents have lost that function . . . the facility to block out high-pitched squeals and screams. Perhaps, genetically, we're supposed to have gone deaf by now so the screams won't bother us.

Here's the thing. There are sentences you don't want to utter to your grandchildren. Here's one:

"Now, now, let's all calm down and play quietly together. Do we have a jigsaw we can all do?"

Almost as bad is someone else coming to your sorry defence:

"Grandad's a little tired. Can we all make a little less noise." *He's an old fart, you see.*

That's your no-fun grandad. Do you want to go down for eternity as a no-fun, let's-be-quiet-children grandfather who is mostly remembered for epitomizing "shush"?

No, me neither.

So I grin and bear it. Sometimes I squeal or scream back, which the kids seem to love but for some inexplicable reason seems to disconcert their parents. I guess a grown man squealing like a pig is disturbing on all kinds of levels.

Sometimes, even grandparents can't hear the squeals. Once, Mayana and I went to a tube park, a place where you ride inner tubes down a snowy hill at breakneck speed. She sat on my lap as I lay spread-eagled on the tube, and we zoomed down the mountain. It was an amazing rush.

When we got to the bottom of the hill, hearts pumping, big smiles on our faces and snow sticking to my beard, Mayana looked at me.

"That was awesome, Grandad."

"Absolutely awesome," I agreed. "I didn't realize it would go quite that fast."

"I know. I was screaming all the way down."

"Were you?" I said. "I didn't hear you at all."

Mayana helped me get out of the tube. "That's because you were screaming louder than me, Grandad." •

The Joke's on Them

One of the greatest things I learned about grandchildren is that they laugh at your jokes. Your kids stopped laughing at your jokes when they were around twelve years old. They still groan. Still accuse you of "dad humour," which means you're lame, out of touch, and totally devoid of anything funny.

But Mayana, during our summer together, laughed at my jokes and asked me to tell her more.

We did knock-knock jokes: *Knock, knock. Who's there? Boo. Boo-who? Don't cry, it's only a joke.* Silly jokes: *What do you call a camel with three humps? I don't know. Humphrey.* She loved to be teased and she laughed and kept me laughing all summer.

There's a lot of laughter when you spend time with a small child. Mostly, they love to be silly, like to pull funny faces, or have you pull them. I became very good at silly walking and dancing, which we'll quickly gloss over here, particularly since I had a sad habit of doing these in public, resulting in some quizzical looks from other adults, suggesting I shouldn't be allowed outside without another grownup.

"I have a joke," Mayana said one afternoon.

"Cool," I said. "Hit me with it."

"Hit you?"

"Just tell me the joke."

She starts giggling.

"Weeeell . . ." she said dragging the word out to three or four syllables.

"Yes?"

"There was this fly . . ."

"Right?"

"And it *flied* away."

She dissolved into gales of laughter, bouncing up and down, and looked for my reaction.

I couldn't help but laugh too. •

6. My Summer with Mayana

[Part Two]

One thing I discovered that summer of 2013 is that an afternoon nap—or quiet time—is absolutely essential for the child. No, strike that . . . for the *grandparent*. Spending time with a three-year-old is beyond exhausting. More exhausting than working, where you can check out or have a break for ten or fifteen minutes.

The most popular sentence uttered by grandparents is, "It's lovely to see the grandchildren, but it's wonderful to give them back."

Grandparenting, apparently, has a time limit. Usually about six hours.

Your grandchild is a massive ball of energy and enthusiasm, crashing into walls and other people, and you're essentially knackered after about four minutes. I have a lot of energy. I play sports. I ski. I bike. I play tennis. But this wasn't the same. There was no downtime.

I'd look after Mayana every day for about ten hours. I resorted to some TV babysitting after breakfast, and we both had an afternoon nap—or quiet time—sometime after lunch. In between she moved at ninety kilometres an hour while I tried to keep up, huffing and puffing.

I know some grandmas who look after a grandchild while the parents are at work, family-based childcare so to speak, and the grandmas hand over the kids at 6:00 p.m. and then they go home to sleep, drained.

The second-most-popular sentence uttered by grandparents is, "If I'd known being a grandparent was going to be this much fun, I'd have had them before I had my kids."

Not at this age you wouldn't. •

TV Time

Television is a superb babysitter. Particularly when you're exhausted. You think you're not going to need TV—you'd probably harrumph and get haughty if your own kids use TV to babysit your grandchild—but after reading three books to your granddaughter and making her breakfast and getting her to brush her teeth and then finding clothes she's willing to wear and socks that match, you're already exhausted beyond belief and need any relief you can get.

Oh, don't get too hoity-toity with me. I know using TV as a babysitter is a cop-out, but sometimes you have to do what you have to do.

I was happy to give Mayana a glass of orange juice, sit her on the sofa, and turn on morning television before we took on the day, while I did the breakfast dishes. But not morning cartoons. One thing I discovered is that TV for kids is a whole lot better than when we grandparents were children. Back then it was all black and white grainy images and awkward puppets with visible strings and adults being incredibly childish or patronizing.

Today, and I'm not exaggerating here, much of TV made for kids is better than much of the TV they're making for adults. There's *Sesame Street*, of course, the good old standby that still helps children spell and sing and learn stuff when they don't realize they're learning.

But there's plenty of other educational stuff masquerading as children's programming. There are science shows, detective shows, animal shows, shows with kids as the heroes and heroines, shows with giants and monsters and aliens, shows with lovable bears— and all of them have people, mostly, being nice to one another. Positive messages and smiling faces light up the screen. This is the exact opposite of prime-time TV, where people are cruel, conniving jerks who will shoot, maim, undermine, or destroy at the drop of a stereotype. And that's just the news. We haven't started with *CSI* yet.

We should all watch more kids' TV. We might learn something.

Mayana loved the *Berenstain Bears*, the animated cartoon based on the picture books created back in 1962 by Stan and Jan Berenstain and, later, their son Mike. An astonishing 250 *Berenstain Bears* books have been published and more than 260 million copies sold.

Mayana also loved the *Berenstain Bears* books, about a family of bears—Mama, Papa, Brother, Sister, and baby Honey—and their many adventures. Grizzly Gran and Gramps show up now and then too, as do their friends and occasional bullies, such as Too Tall. Too Tall can be menacing and scary, but when he's brought down to size he's actually a good kid.

The TV version is true to the books. And there's usually a moral in every story: don't be too greedy; don't envy people their bigger toys; help other people at all times; think of other's feelings; keep a smile on your face. I was hooked on the show.

My favourite story, somewhat ironically for someone who worked in television, is *Too Much TV*, where Mama Bear decides the family has been watching way too much TV. Particularly on sunny days.

The Bear family had once had conversations at the dinner table, but now sat around silently. The young bears didn't go outdoors anymore. So Mama orders the TV to be turned off. For an entire week. It's tough at first, but slowly and surely the Bears start reading and drawing and looking at the stars. Papa is the main problem, however. He tries to sneak downstairs for a peek at the late-night movie. But Mama and the cubs stop him just in time.

The book should be required reading for every parent—and grandparent. And kid.

Some TV is okay. But not too much.

When I wanted us to leave, I'd simply say, "Too Much TV, Mayana." She'd look up, shrug, and say, "Okay."

And we'd put on our shoes and go outside.

If she wanted to do something, go out and play, and I was hooked on PGA golf or a supper-hour newscast, she'd give it right back to me.

"Too Much TV, Grandad."

"Just one more minute . . . I want to see if he makes this putt."

"Grandad."

"Oh, okay."

Click. •

Cabbage Patch Fantasyland

Mayana and I were rooting around in an old trunk when she uncovered them.

"Wow, these are soooo cool, Grandad."

She brandished two floppy dolls with ratty hair . . . both with wide, staring eyes. One blonde, the other a redhead.

"What are they?"

"They," I said grandly, "are Cabbage Patch dolls. They belonged to your mum and auntie. We went through hell to get those for them. They all sold out in a minute."

"Whose was whose?"

"Well, Auntie Jani had the blonde one, because she's blonde, and your mum had the dark-haired one, because she has dark hair."

"Do they have names?"

I wracked my brain. I couldn't remember. After checking with my daughters, we ascertained they were called Sybil Sadie and Rachel Marie.

Mayana loved playing with them. She kept their original names and was thrilled her own mother had also played with them. A friend had some Cabbage Patch doll clothes, so Mayana dressed them up, and enjoyed making up imaginative games. She talked with them a lot.

Mayana also played with an old Barbie doll someone found. I sniffed a little at this, tried to interest her in more gender-neutral games and more upscale, acceptable activities, but she loved the dolls.

She'd also get out stuffed animals and, with the Cabbage Patch dolls and Barbie playing key roles, would put on elaborate shows for me.

I found a book called *365 TV-free Activities*, and we'd do some of them: painting and doing easy quizzes, making bubbles, creating dogs with playdough, and cutting pictures out of magazines.

But the Cabbage Patch dolls, staring and ratty-haired and worse for wear, and Barbie, who was mostly nude, were the summer favourites.

As a grandfather, it mystified me for a while, this compunction to play with dolls, until I realized it had nothing to do with playing mommy or having a pre-school maternal instinct and everything to do with having a vivid imagination.

The dolls were given voices, given little scenarios to act out—mostly pretty minimalist, like going to the park or running away from robbers with accompanying squeals—and they were a means to an end. A means by which to live in a fantasy world. She loved going there. Don't we all. •

Monsters in My Room

There are monsters upstairs.

I figured this out when I asked Mayana to get a sweater from her bedroom. She didn't want to go upstairs on her own—even though the lights were on.

I was fixing supper, a kind of homemade macaroni and cheese with tuna and—for green stuff—frozen peas. It was coagulating in the saucepan. I was thinking I should have bought Kraft Dinner, though I didn't want to serve Mayana cheese the colour of dog barf. Though she'd probably prefer it.

"No, you come with me, Grandad."

"It's okay, Mayana. Your bedroom's just at the top of the stairs. Just run up and get the sweater. It's getting chilly."

And grandad's too cheap to put on the heating. I didn't say this.

"No-o-o." A drawn-out no.

"Why not?"

"There are monsters up there."

Now, none of this made sense. But, as many of you know, not a lot of things make sense when you're dealing with a three-year-old. She had happily slept in this room, and in the dark, for weeks.

"There aren't any monsters up there, sweetie." I said this in a reassuring voice. Okay, with maybe a *hint* of frustration. My macaroni and cheese had turned into a single blob, and I was feverishly drowning it in milk, which wasn't doing any good at all.

"I don't want to go up there. Go with me."

So I took the saucepan off the burner and went to the foot of the stairs. I held her hand and we walked up. Well, she *skipped* up, retrieved a sweater, and skipped down.

"There weren't any monsters, were there? There was nothing to worry about."

"No, they're not there when you're with me."

We left it there. I never did see them. And, later, she seemed to forget all about them too. •

The Dress

Like many men, I'm a sucker for a girl in a dress. That sounds kinda creepy, I know, but when my wife puts on a dress, I'm putty in her hands. A dress is feminine, bright, and beautiful. It's spring and summer. It separates men perfectly from women. We'd look terrible in dresses. That's why we have our short, fat hairy legs, and women have long, smooth, shapely legs. Only a mad, myopic Scotsman would show off his legs under a tartan skirt.

As I write this, I realize how sexist and sad and old-fashioned this all sounds, but I can't help it. A stylish, colourful dress or skirt or posh frock makes me weak in the knees.

I bought my daughters plenty of dresses over the years, though they always preferred jeans and shorts. But every now and then they'd wear them—at Easter or heading off to a summer party—and I'd feel like a million dollars.

They were cute beyond belief. They'd spin and twirl like princesses and seemed to glow. Well, I glowed. I once bought them a couple of dresses when we were in Australia, when they were eight and nine, and they wore them to meet their grandparents for the first time in two years.

"Oh, my, don't you look bonny," said my mum.

"You look like fairy queens," said my dad, and they did. They'd made two old people very happy. Sure, my folks would have been happy if they'd turned up in T-shirts and cut-off jeans, but the dresses were special. They'd put on a show.

Which brings us to the dress in the shop window. Mayana and I saw it while walking along Beacon Avenue in Sidney on Vancouver Island.

Well, I saw it first. It was the most magical dress I'd ever seen. Not too girly or silly, but different. Special.

"Wow, take a look at that dress, Mayana," I said. "What do you think?"

She studied it for a moment.

"Well, it's okay." There was a distinct lack of enthusiasm in her voice. She hadn't learned yet that Grandad was a sucker for dresses.

"Shall we go in?"

"Fine."

Inside, we asked the sales assistant to get it out of the window display for us.

"You have a good eye," she told me.

"What does that mean, Grandad?" said Mayana, squinting at me. "Don't you have two good eyes?"

Once I'd sorted that out, we started examining the dress.

It was called a seaside dress. Handmade. It had straps made of rope, was white on top and blue below. Upon the dress were seaside scenes: an umbrella and beach ball; a palm tree; a sandcastle; a bucket and spade; a sailboat. It was perfect.

Mayana warmed to it too. "I like all the pretty pictures," she said.

She tried on the dress over her shorts and T-shirt. It was a tad big, but we didn't care. "It'll last you next summer too," I said.

She kept it on, and I paid for it—it was pricey but worth every penny—and we went out into the sunshine and she twirled and danced along the street and held her arms out wide.

"I love it," I said.

"I think I love it too," said Mayana. We drew admiring glances as she skipped along the street and I beamed.

She'll wear plenty of dresses in her lifetime. Dresses for parties, dresses for dress-up, dresses for Halloween, dresses for graduation, but that dress will always be burned into my memory. Better than any fancy-schmancy dress on any red carpet anywhere.

A million-dollar dress? That dress was worth a billion. •

The Ring

"Look at what I got for Mommy, Grandad."

Mayana had something clutched in her hand. We had just been to see an IMAX movie on space exploration that she had pronounced "awesome," and now we were getting into the car.

"What is it, Mayana?"

"It's a present. Mommy said she was going to get me a gift this weekend, so I got her one too."

"That's nice," I said as I drove the car through heavy traffic. I glanced in the rear-view mirror. "What is it?"

"A ring," she said, and held it up for me to see. I couldn't see it clearly, but it looked like a cheap ring that she must have found in her pocket or in the back of the car, where, frankly, there's enough random detritus to fill a junk shop.

When we got home, she showed me the ring again.

It was the ugliest ring I had ever seen. It had three skulls, one larger, two smaller, on either side. It was ghoulish, terrifying, and dark.

"It's beautiful, isn't it, Grandad?"

"It's, er, very nice. Where on earth did you get it?"

"At the IMAX. After the show. I found it."

"On the floor?"

"No, I found it . . . it was in a box. On a shelf. In that gift shop."

Oh! My sweet little granddaughter was a shoplifter.

The gift shop and the IMAX is actually part of the Royal BC Museum, and I was mystified why they'd be selling rings that would have been more suited to trinkets at a Hell's Angels convention.

"How do you mean it was on a box on a shelf? Like, for sale?"

"No, it was just in a box in the corner."

I'm not sure how I missed her taking the ring. We had walked hand-in-hand back to the car, and I had buckled her into her seat. Maybe she was wearing it. I'm a trained observer. A journalist. But I miss things.

Let's go back sixty years or so, to a small arcade in the seaside town of Southend-on-Sea in England. The arcade had a bazaar-like atmosphere, full of market stalls, with goods on display. My mother and I were walking around aimlessly. I loved the happy chaos of the place. Mum briefly let go of my hand to pore over some bargain shoes at one stall.

The adjoining stall was full of toys. To a toddler it was an absolute inviting array of brightly coloured toys and games. Yo-yos and toy soldiers and kites and dolls and cars and ribbons and balloons.

And rubber tomahawks.

There, in a box at the front of the stall, were at least twenty of them. All tacky and, nowadays, as inappropriate as the toy guns next to them—and more politically incorrect. But I couldn't resist touching one. I picked it up. It had a red handle and a silver, realistic-looking blade. I tried a few random practice *whacks* and loved it. I immediately put it in my raincoat pocket.

I had to have it. I'm not sure if my mother had already turned me down when I'd pleaded for some other toy or treat—meaning there was no chance she'd buy me a rubber tomahawk—but the act was intentional and full of subterfuge. I knew it was wrong to take it. But I couldn't help myself.

Later, as we took the bus home, I kept patting it in my pocket. Ready to scalp at an instant.

When we got home, I took it out of my pocket and started waving it about at my sister. My dad asked what I was doing.

"Playing with my tomahawk."

"Where'd you get that, then?"

"At the arcade in Southend."

My mother turned towards me. "Did you take it from that toy stall? I thought you looked guilty."

I didn't even try and lie.

"All right," said my mum. "You know it's wrong to take things without paying, don't you?"

"Er, um, well . . ."

My mother told me to put my raincoat back on, and we went outside into a gloomy afternoon, waited for the bus, then took a twenty-minute ride back to the arcade. I was made to go up to the stall, tell the owner what I'd done, apologize, and give the tomahawk back.

The owner had a wry smile on his face, but my mother painstakingly explained why it was wrong—that I was taking something that didn't belong to me, which meant that the stall owner would lose money. The way my mother told the story the poor man wouldn't be able to eat again and would have to live in a tent because I'd damaged his livelihood. She may have also mentioned the police and jail and throwing away the key.

Here's the thing: I never shoplifted again in my life—not even when school friends were pocketing chocolate bars or licorice chews when the shop owner's back was turned. It never felt right.

So Mayana and I got back in the car, drove the thirty minutes south to Victoria, parked in the same parking lot and went back to the gift shop and told the clerk that we'd—*we'd!*—taken the ring by mistake. And apologized.

"I'm not sure we sell that ring," said the clerk, sniffily. He began hunting around, and then found a small box of cheap knickknacks. "Oh, I guess it came from there. They're awful, aren't they? I'm not sure why we sell them."

We put the ring in the box, and I grandly told Mayana why it was wrong to take something without paying.

"Oh, I already know that," said Mayana. "I just forgot I had the ring until I realized I had it in the car."

"Well, isn't that convenient, just forgetting like that," said the clerk, somewhat sarcastically.

I instantly disliked him and wanted to punch him in his Gen Z nose. Lucky for him I'm steadfastly anti-violence. And a coward.

We didn't buy the ring. We bought a small bag of pretty stones instead so that she could give one each to everyone in the family.

"I don't have any money, Grandad," she said.

I paid.

As we left the store, she waved the receipt at me. "See, it's proof we paid for it."

I'm not sure the message got through fully. I was still ticked off at the store clerk. I thought of telling her that next time she wanted to swipe a ring, she should choose Tiffany's.

Instead, I asked if she knew what a tomahawk was. •

What I Learned That Summer ————————————————

Crosby, Stills & Nash told us to teach our children well. But what do you teach your granddaughter? Whose values? Old-fashioned values formed when you were a child in the 1950s, where girls were fluffy and light and wore pretty dresses? Sixties values of peace and love and dropping out? Glitter rock values? That no good music was made after 1969, with the exception of Nirvana and Pearl Jam and Cat Stevens and *Bridge over Troubled Water*?

The thing is, you're rapidly out of date the moment your grandchild is born. Your job is to be out of date, representing history rather than relevance.

So when you speak of Carnaby Street or the Summer of Love or the Beatles or Twiggy or JFK or RFK or Nixon and Watergate or, in fact, absolutely anything that happened before the year 2010, you are simply talking another language.

The fact your granddaughter sings "Yellow Submarine" in her car seat is an anachronism. It doesn't mean anything. It's "The Wheels on the Bus." It's not validation. You are an artefact. An antique. That's your job.

And don't hum any Lady Gaga or Ed Sheeran. Remember when your parents went, "yeah, yeah, yeah" to show they knew who the Beatles were? You will be that pathetic.

Teach your grandchildren well. How to say please and thank you, how to look both ways before they cross the road. How to be kind and how to be polite and how to stay safe. How to help others. And share.

Answer their questions.

The meaning-of-life, important stuff? Leave that to Mum and Dad.

I tried to teach Mayana a few things that summer, but I learned more than I taught. I learned magical things. I learned that being a grandparent is a special relationship that's difficult to explain.

Being a parent was a whole lot of fun too, something I still enjoy, but when the kids were younger there was also the stress of daily life to go through, bills to pay (don't start playing "Cat's in the Cradle"), and sometimes you didn't stop as often as you should have to enjoy those memorable moments.

When you get older, you're forced to slow down. And because you know your life is rushing along at break-neck speed, you know every moment is precious.

Or as Mayana might have said back then, "Time to smell the chriscinnamons." •

7. You're Going Grey and Very Hairy, Grandad

Emma is quite the artist. She's creative and daring and will give David Hockney a run for his money soon. She just did this amazing portrait of my wife. Nani looks—how do I put this delicately?— much younger than she really is. She has dark rather than grey hair, huge friendly eyes, a cute button nose, and the biggest smile on the planet. That part is accurate. My wife's smile would launch a thousand kayaks. That's how Emma sees her Nani, as young and vibrant and happy.

Then Emma drew me.

"Stay still, Grandad."

I put on my George Clooney face, that one with the ironic smile and the warm, craggy eyes, and then she said, far too early I thought, "Finished."

And I was a skinhead. "I look like a bovver boy," I said.

"What's a bovver boy, Grandad?"

"Well, a bovver boy," I explained, "was a young hoodlum in Britain in the seventies."

"That's just about right," said my daughter Jani, who had been observing from the sidelines.

I tried to be encouraging. "I like the red hair, though I think my hair is more brown."

"It's grey, Grandad, but I couldn't find any grey felts."

"And the eyes are very nice but seem a little beady, and my nose looks threatening."

"Yes," said Emma.

"Yes what?"

"Yes, that's just about right."

My beard was scraggly and took up most of my face. Which, on reflection, is pretty accurate.

"I love it," I told her, and I do.

It's on the fridge now, below Nani's, alongside pictures of all of our grandkids and calendars and assorted bric-a-brac.

Fridges have become grandparents' art galleries. Their kids' art used to be there, and now it's their grandkids' paintings and drawings. Mostly rainbows and unicorns and incomprehensible Picasso-esque pieces that we will cherish forever.

Even if Grandad is now immortalized as a skinhead.

Your ego certainly takes a beating when you have grandkids. They have no filter.

Sometimes Mayana likes to brush my hair. And like all good hair-dressers, she's not short of conversation.

"Why is your hair so grey, Grandad?"

"Because your mum made me old," I said. "I earned every one of them."

"Huh?"

"It's a joke. You'll understand when you're older."

"Does grey hair mean you're old?"

"Sorta."

"Why do you have more grey hairs in your beard than you have on your head?"

"Well, your Nani says it's because I talk a lot and don't think a lot. So the hair around my mouth has done a lot more work than the hair on my head. It got older quicker."

"Is that true, Grandad?"

"Maybe. She might be right. She usually is."

"Why do you have hair growing out of your ears?"

"I'm not sure."

"They're grey too."

"Well, I guess I've done a lot of listening over the years. Maybe I've earned them."

"But why do you have hair growing out of your ears? I don't. Mummy doesn't. My daddy doesn't either."

"It happens when you get older. Hair starts growing in all kinds of places it never grew before. And for no reason. And it stops growing where it used to grow, like on the top of your head."

"Where else is it growing?"

"Well, all kinds of places. Like my nose. I have hair up my nose."

"Let me look . . . oh, yes, but not too many."

"I trim them. I have a nose-hair trimmer. I never thought I'd ever need a nose-hair trimmer, but there you go."

"Do you trim your ears too?"

"I try."

"You're not very good at it, are you?"

"No. It's easier to see up your nose in the mirror than in your ears. I use a pair of scissors. I use a beard trimmer. I even shave my ears. I never thought I'd shave my ears."

"Do you ever cut yourself when you shave your ears?"

"I did once. I nicked my earlobe. I didn't realize I had. Then I was at work, in a meeting, a big sort of important meeting, and someone came over to me and whispered, 'Your ear's bleeding.' And it was. I had blood dripping onto my shirt collar."

"Yeeeeuch."

"Yeah, that's almost exactly what everyone in the meeting said. I told them it was bleeding because I couldn't bear to listen to all the rubbish they were speaking."

"Ha ha."

"Mayana, why are you combing my hair forward over my face? I can't see anything."

"It looks nice like this. Do you want me to cut it for you too?"

"No, that's okay. I'd like to live a few more years."

"I can just cut out the grey hairs."

"No, that's fine. They're part of me now. What colour are the hairs that aren't grey?"

"Hmmmm. Kinda brown."

"But there's lots of hair up there, right?"

"Not as much as I have."

"Wrong answer. Hairdressers always say, 'You have lovely hair, sir. Very thick and healthy for someone your age.'"

"Do they really say that?"

"Yes."

"Why?"

"Because I pay them lots of money."

"Great. Your hair looks very lovely, sir. Beautiful. Wonderful."

"Thank you. Don't overdo it."

"Do you give me money now?"

"Sure. Here's five cents."

"Thank you."

"Now can your brush the hair out of my eyes. I'd like to see what I look like."

Musical and Magical

Art and music figure a lot in children's lives. They draw pictures, sing songs and dance around with gay abandon and then, for some mysterious reason, when they get older they just stop. Not all of them, obviously, but most. They lose their inner creativity and become boring grownups, self-conscious observers rather than participants.

A love of music, and making music, is something I wanted to pass on to both my kids and grandkids. It's a joy for life. I am, unashamedly, a populist when it comes to music. Mainstream has usually been my mantra, though I enjoy venturing into other genres when forced to. Even these are pretty safe choices—easy classical, folk, and Celtic music, and even some random rap or hip-hop so I can pretend I'm not some boring, middle-of-the-road, cardigan-wearing old fart. In my defence, I once went to Seattle and wrote a feature story on the grunge music phenomenon and have since enjoyed Pearl Jam and Nirvana very much, if not often.

My wife and I—grandparents that we are—went to an Ed Sheeran concert in London last year and stood up and clapped and sang along with sixty thousand other fans who were mostly decades younger than us. It made me feel strangely young. And very old. That said, his music works for just about anybody. Midway through his show he brought on a special guest. The previous evening it had been Andrea Bocelli, so I expected a similar mainstream, perhaps light operatic, delight. Instead we got Stormzy, a British rapper. Stormzy's Wikipedia profile says he "garnered attention on the UK underground music scene through his Wicked Skengman series of freestyles over classic grime beats." Yup, I'm totally into grime beats.

Mostly, at this concert, we revelled in the fact that Sheeran was decades younger than many of the previous performers we had seen: James Taylor, Gordon Lightfoot (who began his concert saying reports of his death had been greatly exaggerated), and Leonard Cohen, who has since died but still out-hips just about everyone onstage today.

As I write this, I realize I haven't been to many major concerts over the past few years. I guess grandfathers don't go out so much. I used to be a rock critic and interviewed and reviewed a whole slew of acts—mostly in the seventies and eighties, so I certainly got my fill.

As a young kid I saw the Beatles, the Stones, the Who, the Kinks, and just about all of the British Invasion stars, and some fun lesser-known bands too, like the Fingers and Swinging Blue Jeans.

I got to see Elvis, the Eagles, Supertramp, Phil Collins, the older Stones, Genesis, Beach Boys, and Elton John. I even interviewed Frank Zappa (we got on famously). Some regrets: I never got to see Simon and Garfunkel, though my wife did before we met and never fails to bring it up when I start going down this kind of musical memory lane. I didn't see Springsteen and, my biggest regret of all, never got to see Linda Ronstadt live. I'm now fanatical—the true sense of "fan" and enjoy her on YouTube. The tragedy is that because of Parkinson's, we will never hear her sing live again. She is very philosophical about it in interviews and is still adorable.

I've also been immensely proud of, and enjoyed, Canadian music over the years. Lightfoot's "If You Could Read My Mind" is still one of the most haunting folk songs ever written. Joni Mitchell is a goddess. Stan Rogers, k.d. lang, the Barenaked Ladies, Blue Rodeo, Neil Young, Bryan Adams, Michael Bublé, Drake, the McGarrigle sisters, Justin Bieber, Rufus Wainwright, Sarah McLachlan, Diana Krall, Arcade Fire, the Tragically Hip, Bruce Cockburn, Murray McLachlan, the Band, Rush, Crash Test Dummies, Stompin' Tom Connors, April Wine, Celine Dion, Buffy Sainte-Marie, Shania Twain. I mean—that's an unbelievable lineup. And that's off the top of my head.

Okay—so let's get to the point. Does any of this matter to my kids or grandkids? Does the music I love matter a damn to them? Or, like old books, is it best kept hidden in the echoes of my mind? (See what I did there?)

Well, like just about everything else, some of it will get through, some of it won't, and that's just fine. But to me, music is a critically important part of who I am. I like to play guitar and piano, and I love to sing, even if I can clear a room in thirty seconds.

When I grew up, my dad had a musical bent. He could play mandolin and some basic piano, and he'd sing along to old 78 rpm records, He particularly enjoyed Gilbert and Sullivan, and my enduring memory of him is when he sang his favourite song from The Gondoliers, namely "Take a Pair of Sparkling Eyes." I can still, to this day, hear his voice so clearly.

So yes, my father's music rubbed off on me, and I know my music rubbed off on my kids because I inflicted it on them at every turn. I sang them into submission. I became a poor man's Raffi and Fred Penner at campfire singalongs, and sometimes sang at their kindergartens and playschools, and encouraged them to sing wherever and whenever.

They found their own music, which was mostly rubbish—and still is, if my younger son's car playlist is anything to go by. He even likes country music, which I kind of get because he lived in Alberta for two years and that's all they play on radio there. I like Keith Urban and Shania Twain, and I did like Willie Nelson a lot but—well, that's about it. It's like jazz. If you love it, you're a sociopathic addict. If you can take it or leave it, aficionados look upon you as a music cretin.

Since, at the time of writing, my grandkids are ten, six and four, their tastes vary wildly ... and by the week. In their very early years, Emma and Linden loved the Wiggles, the Australian children's group who do highly entertaining shows—on screen and live. The Wiggles, on iPad, helped us keep both of them amused on long trips and in restaurants where the service was slower than the kids' patience.

For a long time, Emma—aged about two—loved "All About That Bass," by Meghan Trainor. She sang it repeatedly and danced around, and I kind of liked it. I'm not so sure Emma ever understood the lyrics, which celebrate plus-size women, but I guess my granddaughter was ahead of her time, socially speaking.

More recently, Emma was addicted to JoJo Siwa, a YouTube sensation who sings, dances, and acts in videos that go instantly viral and earn her bazillions. She tells kids to be their true selves and be proud of who they are. Which sounded to me like an updated Mr. Rogers. I liked the message but found her a little irritating. So did Emma, apparently. After two weeks or so she moved on to the Next Big Thing.

Linden is a little less selective. He had me play "Baa, Baa, Black Sheep" on piano about ten thousand times while he bounced around the living room.

"What do you want this time, Linden?"

"Black Sheep, Grandad. Black Sheep."

"How about 'Twinkle, Twinkle, Little Star?'" (Same tune.)

"Black Sheep, Grandad." I hate that song.

Mayana isn't shy about singing, and at age ten seems to know who's hot this week and can sing most songs out loud. She, Emma, and I do "Castle on a Cloud" from *Les Misérables*, with me on piano and the girls singing the sad little song together.

When my kids were very young, they all enjoyed Raffi. I played guitar and learned most of his songs, and we'd sing them often.

The kids hated folk music, mostly because we did a family house clean every Saturday morning, and I'd put this folk music show on the radio. I loved it, but they equated cleaning with Celtic music, and "Dust in the Wind" became a cruel metaphor for their Saturday morning despair.

Tim was into Metallica, and still is. Paul liked Korn and then Smash Mouth. He also played the local hard-rock Fox channel, recorded the songs, and then did his own DJing. Now he's a broadcaster. Figures. In high school Jani was into Blind Melon, Counting Crows, Pearl Jam, and Our Lady Peace. Eldest daughter Amy now sings in public from time to time. She remembers dancing to Mike Oldfield's "Moonlight Shadow," one of my favourite songs, repeatedly in the living room.

My memory of both girls is them singing "Tomorrow" from the musical *Annie* so often on a road trip through Ontario and the Maritimes that I wanted to jump out of the car. It was wonderful the first time. But that's the thing with young children . . . they just never let go. They discover a song, it becomes an earworm, and then they sing it until they—and you—are blue in the face. To their credit, they also knew just about every song from *Les Misérables*. We had been to see it together and they regaled us with the French revolution for three full weeks.

They also sing for me, on many birthdays, "Song for a Winter's Night," by Gordon Lightfoot. They sing in perfect harmony.

On my last landmark birthday, as a surprise, my family booked a party bus and we went on a musical mystery tour. The bus was festooned with balloons and banners, and the sound system, for four hours, belted out Beatles and such—and the odd Ed Sheeran—while we all sang along at the top of our voices.

And when we got to "Yellow Submarine" they could hear us a mile away. Musical and magical. But not so much a mystery. Music, thank God, is in our bones. Even if sometimes we get a little out of tune. •

Bedtime Stories

"Dogger. Dogger. Dogger."

That was Mayana at bedtime. We would read a story every night, before she went to sleep when I was taking care of her, and almost every night it was *Dogger*.

Dogger is my favourite kids' book. I read it to my own kids. And we found an old, moth-eaten copy that belonged to my youngest son, Paul—his name's still in it in red marker-pen—and that's what we read again and again and again.

I won't spoil the story for you by telling you how it ends, but it's a beautifully told little story about a little boy who loved his stuffed dog, how he loses it, and how his older sister tries to get it back for him.

It's beautifully illustrated by Shirley Hughes, very English working-class, and you have a heart of granite if you're not misty eyed by the final page.

Mayana never tired of it. Or, for that matter, any of the regular rotation of books that we read together, from *Berenstain Bears* through *Goldilocks* through *Winnie the Pooh*.

Again, Grandad.

Again.

Young kids love repetition. And they are comforted by familiar things.

We adults are easily bored. Even sleepy, when we read to our grandkids (I actually started snoring one night while reading to Mayana). We want something new and fresh and interesting.

Kids like the new. But when it comes to literature and songs, they want what they know.

I hesitate to recommend books to other grandparents because I find they all have their favourites. Usually a book they read as a child, or as a parent. Something that defines their culture, or interests, or who and what they are. And they love sharing those books with their grandkids.

But *Dogger* is something special. You'll see.

Another popular bedtime story in our family—or a series of them, rather—revolves around the adventures of Sidney the Squirrel. Sidney is a forgetful squirrel. I invented him one night when putting one of my grandkids to bed. I forget which one.

Sidney lives with his parents and sister in a tree in the wood, and always forgets things. He forgets to take his lunch to school, forgets to pick up shopping, forgets to wear his jacket. He forgets just about anything I can think of as the story progresses.

This is no *Watership Down*, with deep, meaningful bits. It's just Sidney the forgetful squirrel tying a string around his paw to remember something and then forgetting why he put the string there in the first place. And so on.

The grandkids like it. "Ohhhhhh Sidney," they'll say. "Not again ..." whenever he forgets a message or a bottle of milk.

Sometimes, Mayana or Emma will ask me to tell them two Sidney stories in the same night, which is way too stressful. But I try. Some Sidney stories are better than others, some are embarrassingly bad. But they're our stories. Something we share. Linden likes them too.

Which is all well and good ... except when one of the grandchildren asks me to tell them a story I'd told before. An elaborate story. "You know, Grandad, the one when Sidney forgot his homework."

"Ah yes," I'll say, having entirely forgotten the first story. "Just remind me a little bit, okay?" •

Birthdays

Birthdays have always been a big deal in our family. Not when I was a kid, though. I can remember eating jelly and blancmange, a terrible concoction that sounds exotic (in French: *eat white*) but is essentially jelly mixed with milk and sugar. We played a couple of perfunctory games, ate some, felt sick some, and then went home.

By the time our kids were young, parties had become much more elaborate affairs, with lots of other kids, plenty of food, homemade cakes, and various themes. We had a magic party for Jani where, with Amy as my assistant, we did a basic magic show. I think Jani's friends were about six, so wonderfully gullible. My best trick had me making a ten-dollar note that I'd burned in front of them reappear in the middle of a halved-lemon. My party piece, literally. It had a somewhat sad ending when the smoke alarms went off and the parents arrived to pick up the little darlings while they were running around, screaming. It was only a little smoke, for Pete's sake.

We had a skating party for Amy on a school pro-d day and invited all the kids in Grade 1. We lived next door to the ice rink and ordered pizza, so it was pretty easy. Except I had to help tie about thirty pairs of skates. I owe my back many apologies.

And we had a pirate party for Paul. He was three, I think. This meant hiking him and his friends down onto a beach to look for treasure that we'd hidden. Beth led them as they sang happily all along the path. Then Amy, Jani, Tim, and I, dressed as pirates and carrying wooden swords, leaped out of the bushes, shouted "Aaaargh" and such, and the little pirates turned and ran screaming back up the hill.

"You didn't have to be quite so authentic," said my wife once we'd recovered and returned the jabbering wrecks to the beach.

My grandkids' parties are even more impressive. Elsa and Anna from *Frozen* have been hired for a backyard party for Emma. They were two local actresses who stayed in character the whole party. Every other little girl was dressed in costume too. There was also a bouncy castle—how did we manage before bouncy castles? There were hot dogs and hummus and avocado dip and beer and wine. These last drinks were for the adults, who stayed. That's a big difference. Parents never used to stay at parties. Now, more often than not, they stick around. A good thing. You need all the help you can get.

Sometimes, when Emma was very small, I was asked to sing some Raffi songs on guitar. The singing went quite well until I realized the kids had wandered off to play elsewhere while all the moms were sitting down and joining in. This was their music. They knew all the words.

My daughter and son-in-law have rented the local rec centre's gym, where the kids can play with hoops and pedal cars and such, and then have pizza. They have been to parties where they make crafts, take over local parks, and play dress-up, where the kids are space monsters or dinosaurs or fairies. A friend of mine tells me his small grandchild had a Sgt. Pepper party where all the kids dressed up like mini-Beatles. I'm still envious.

Our grandkids seem to go to parties just about every weekend, sometimes more than one. I can honestly remember going to just four or five actual birthday parties when I was a child. I'm not sure if kids had them or—and this pains me—I just wasn't invited. Mostly, we had birthday cake and the aforementioned blancmange with our family at home. I know I blew out plenty of candles, but that stopped in my teenage years. Now I'd prefer them to leave the candles off the cake. It's becoming more of a sad inferno every year. •

One in Seven Billion

Sometimes when I'm looking after them I'll tiptoe into my grandkids' rooms and look at them while they are sleeping. It's something I used to do when my own kids were small. There's nothing as beautiful or serene as a child asleep.

I look at them and think they are the most special children on the planet. Which to me at that precise moment, they are.

But here's the thing. Grandparents around the world are doing exactly the same thing.

In global terms, my grandkids aren't one in a million. But one in more than seven billion. That's the population of this planet. We are but a grain of sand, an ant, an insignificant, irrelevant speck on the face of the earth.

Or are we?

It's easy to get lost in all the noise. Seven billion people can make a lot of noise. Just turn on the TV . . . there's a lot of noise out there, much of it ugly, much of it scary.

That seven billion figure is striking some fear into the planet. How many more people can fit on this globe swirling around the universe?

Will the earth be able to feed, water, clothe, and house all these people in the future?

Probably not. A whole bunch of the earth's inhabitants go to bed at night sparsely dressed and desperately hungry as they gaze up at those distant stars.

It's good that the media, scientists, and sociologists are examining all the ramifications of population growth right now, at this significant stage in the history of earth. The media will focus on human consumption, carbon footprints, and myriad population issues.

But it's not the mass of humanity we should focus on.

It's the power of the individual. The human story.

Or, as we say in the media, the human-interest story.

Estimates vary wildly, but somewhere between thirty and ninety billion humans have walked on this planet since time—well, earth's time—began. There would be a lot of bones beneath that earth if most hadn't disintegrated by now. From dust to dust. Dust in the wind.

I can't work out what seven billion people looks like. The mind boggles. I can imagine sixty thousand people in a stadium. Maybe a hundred thousand. But the mind can't really countenance billions of people.

It's not the mass of humanity that's the story, it's the small yet heroic stories that are important. We *Homo sapiens* are a ruggedly individual bunch—not blank faces in the crowd, but individuals with fascinating individual and complex personalities.

Good and bad. Happy and sad. Heroic and cowardly. Ambitious and meek. Leaders and followers. Athletic and clumsy. Gifted and dull. Nerds and ne'er-do-wells. And we all got to be born, as Buffy Sainte-Marie once sang, by the skin of our teeth.

When I was in the news business, we did the big stories—but tried to balance them with small stories. We hunted for the human-interest stories, the tales of ordinary people, to relate the bigger issues. To help us all find a connection, to make you care. Because you do.

Thousands of people died on 9/11, but it was the individual stories of courage and tragedy that inspired and helped us understand. The falling man story. The "let's roll" story. The photograph on the fence of the missing husband or daughter. And how often have we been transfixed by TV images of the miracle of a child being pulled alive from the rubble of an earthquake or other natural disaster? We can relate to the individual. Not always to the mass.

When I was a young reporter, I was often sent to the homes of accident victims to get a photo to illustrate the story.

Some reporters hated hitting the doorsteps of the grieving, but I told victims' relatives and friends that I wanted to tell a story about a human being. Not a statistic. I often used to get the picture.

I believed it then, I believe it now. Movies tell big, sweeping epics with smaller, human dramas. Rhett and Scarlett in *Gone with the Wind*. Kate and Leonardo's characters in *Titanic*. The anonymous tragic little girl in red in *Schindler's List,* or Roberto Benigni's wonderful father in *Life Is Beautiful*.

Millions died in the Second World War, but we can still cry for the fate of the individual, the girl in the red dress. We can still care about that speck of sand.

We have the capacity to love and to hate, to laugh and cry. We are ecstatic when a baby is born, particularly when it's part of our family. We treasure its first moments and marvel at how it grows from a tiny speck into a beautiful child.

Tomorrow, babies will be born in every corner of the planet. Most, if they are lucky, will come into a world where they will be loved and cherished and nurtured on the road to the most miraculous journey of them all.

Life.

Even with a population of seven billion, we all count.

Children and grandchildren remind us of our own mortality. But they also remind us that each of us is vital and beautiful. In our very small way. Watch your grandchild sleep, and you'll know what I mean. •

8. An Early Christmas Gift

Linden was an early Christmas gift. But he was still put on hold so my daughter Jani could go to a party.

Okay, the party bit isn't quite as hedonistic as it sounds. Linden was due a week before Christmas, when we were due to have an early Christmas with our family. Twenty-one of us. Twenty-one! Because we're a large family, with kids, partners, aunts, uncles, cousins, and assorted hangers-on (some of whom I barely recognize) we do Christmas when we can. Actually, we do *anything* when we can. Bringing us all together for Thanksgiving, Easter, Father's Day, Mother's Day, or family picnics takes military planning and a lot of flexibility. One year, for reasons I've now forgotten, we swapped Mother's Day with Father's Day, and my wife fell and banged her head and dislocated her finger when hiking on a beach, so we're not doing that again. You don't mess with the natural order of things.

But Christmas? It's a moveable feast. Paul is a broadcaster now and often works on Christmas Day, and our kids' partners—for some self-indulgent reason—want to visit their own parents sometimes at Christmas, and so when we can't do Christmas on December 25, we do it earlier. I once did a Christmas with my sisters in England on Remembrance Day, which was beyond surreal. Sombre reflection and ho-ho-hos aren't a good combination.

So my daughter, who was to be induced—I'm not quite sure what that means, but it apparently involves walking up and downstairs a lot to get things moving. Though I could be wrong; I'm not a doctor. Anyway, she asked if it was a problem if she delayed things to the Sunday rather than the Saturday, and they said it'd be fine if she were careful and didn't go crazy, and so she came to the party.

A party that was, actually, quite something. We have a large building in our backyard that houses kayaks and camping gear and other stuff, but my wife and I secretly transformed it into a winter wonderland, complete with trees, lights, tables, and music. Only Mayana was in on the secret. We gathered in our family room, cheek-by-jowl, and had drinks and nibbles, and it was Jani who twigged to the circumstances. Mainly because she was sober.

"So where are we eating?" she asked. And then she answered her own question. "On our laps, I guess, since there are so many of us."

At 5:00 p.m. we told everyone to put on their shoes, and Mayana would lead them outside.

"Where are we going?" asked my brother-in-law. "To the picnic table? It's gonna be freezing."

Mayana led us via a line of candles into the back room, and it was spectacular. There were some tears. We ate, played silly games, laughed a lot, I played piano, and we sang "The Twelve Days of Christmas," which always ends in a collapse of laughter.

"Okay," said Jani as the evening subsided, "I think I'll go and have my baby now."

And she did. We looked after Emma, and she and her husband, Chris, went to the hospital the next morning while the rest of the family had an early Boxing Day. And then Chris called and said, "You have a grandson," and we all trooped off to the hospital—children and grandchildren—and invaded the maternity ward with balloons and cards and food.

"We picked you up a burger and fries en route," we told Chris, because he'd said he was starving.

"Where's mine?" said Jani, cradling her new son. "I pop a baby and suddenly I'm chopped liver."

We told her we'd thought she'd be eating hospital food.

"Seriously?" she said.

"Seriously."

In the end, she stole some of Chris's.

Oh yes. Linden. Probably the cutest baby in the universe at that precise moment. Lots of hair again—it's a trend in our family—and a puffy little face and, well, I could tell he was going to become a matinée idol. Eventually.

We passed him among us, all taking turns to hold and love him and oooh and aaah and all the usual stuff. I checked he had all his fingers and toes and remarked on how small they were, which is what you do, and then had to hand him on.

"Welcome to the chaos, kid," I said. "Welcome to the family."

I love Christmas, always have, and as a grandfather I seem to enjoy it even more . . . perhaps because with every passing year I increasingly resemble Santa Claus.

Part of that enjoyment is the memory of Christmases past. By the time you become a grandparent, you're fortunate enough to have witnessed many Christmases, as a child, as a teenager, as an adult, as a spouse, a father, and then as a grandfather. You've seen *It's a Wonderful Life* and *A Christmas Carol* so often you can recite most of the lines. And you've heard Bing Crosby sing "White Christmas" so often that you're surprised the final line still leaves a lump in your throat.

While we're on Christmas music, I'm a sucker for "In the Bleak Midwinter" and "Silent Night," both carols showing how much emotion can be evoked by gentle music.

I pretend I'm somewhat outraged by the fact some easy listening radio stations start playing carols in late November, and then find myself switching to them repeatedly. Until Paul McCartney starts singing "Wonderful Christmastime" and I realize enough is enough. He may be one of the greatest songwriters of all time, but he could still produce his fair share of yuletide schlock.

I have been lucky enough to have had a few white Christmases, when we lived in Ottawa, and when as a family we have headed to ski hills for the holidays. I've also had a few hot Christmases, in Hawaii, Mexico, and Australia, but don't enjoy them as much as I probably should. Well, in Mexico, I always get sick. So that figures. There's not much ho ho ho or Christmas magic around when you're spending most of your time hovering over a toilet bowl.

But there's something incongruous about sun and Christmas. Which is why I like grey Christmases most of all. I had grey Christmases as a child growing up in England, and that's what I usually get on the West Coast of Canada. Not rain. I like to go out for walks on Christmas Day, but not huddled under an umbrella.

But that's the point of Christmas. It is tradition and it is memory.

I remember being a child and loving the family warmth of Christmas. Mostly, I remember my parents and how welcoming they were. We were a big family anyway, in a small English council house, but that didn't stop my mum inviting every waif and stray for Christmas dinner.

"Ooooh," she'd say, "I met this poor woman yesterday, and she had nowhere to go for Christmas dinner. Can you imagine that? So I've invited her over."

And a few others too.

Our kitchen table wasn't big enough for more than four people, so Dad would take a door off by the hinges, place it on top of the smaller table and we'd sit in the middle of the living room and pull Christmas crackers and laugh and go "ooooh" at the Christmas pudding, when it was lit up with brandy.

If memory serves, we never did have turkey, but a large chicken full of stuffing and surrounded by sausages and bacon, and served with delicious roast potatoes and sprouts, which none of the kids liked that much, mostly because in those days cooking vegetables amounted to boiling them within an inch of their lives so that they became a mushy, watery, inedible slop. But we covered it all in gravy, and the kids were allowed to sip Babycham, a low-alcohol champagne perry (like cider but made with pears), and it was, well, spectacular. We wore our paper hats extracted from the Christmas crackers, and read our riddles—Why does Santa have three gardens? So he can hoe-hoe-hoe—and we played with our small compasses or key rings or other cracker toys.

One year, on a whim, my mother decided we'd have a goose for Christmas, which was very daring and also quite posh for a working-class family. All morning she complained that while roasting it was making an awful lot of fat, and by lunchtime—in England, most Christmas dinners are eaten at midday—the goose was cooked and proudly brought to the table. My father beamed as he took the carving knife and fork, inserted it into the bird . . .

And sprayed all of us with goose fat, as it spurted for what seemed an eternity. We mopped our clothes, our faces, our hair, and started laughing our heads off.

"Bit fatty, that bird," said Dad. "But it looks very moist."

My mum was reassured it was the best bird ever (certainly the most memorable) and we loved every bite. The next year, we went back to chicken.

Now, Christmases are spent with kids and grandkids, and it's still the most magical time of the year, and stressful and busy and, suddenly, it's all over before it's started. We're fortunate if we have family to share it with. It's a time to be kinder, less mean, less self-absorbed. •

The Grandfather Clause

Here are some thoughts on Santa Claus that I once expounded in the Victoria *Times Colonist*.

Santa is sitting in our living room, dispensing gifts to neighbourhood children, and saying to a young boy, "So what do you want for Christmas, man?"

Man? This is Groovy Santa, who, if you look beneath the expensive red Santa suit, shiny black boots, white hair and beard, bears a striking resemblance to my eldest son, Tim.

Tim is a big lad, but a large pillow is still necessary for the required girth.

Groovy Santa is also Virgin Santa. This is a maiden performance. And an impressive one.

Not that Tim hasn't been pressed into service at Christmas before. He played a shepherd in the kindergarten nativity scene, wearing a tea towel over his head, if memory serves.

He played trumpet in the middle-school band Christmas concert, and we puffed with pride until we discovered he wasn't actually blowing into the instrument, but miming. "I was afraid I'd mess up 'Good King Wenceslas,'" he confessed. "It's really difficult."

Every year, poor Tim has to do a Dickensian Tiny Tim and say, "God bless us everyone," before Christmas dinner because it's a tradition. He said it when he was really tiny and now Christmas isn't Christmas without it. It's kind of kitsch now, and he probably wishes we'd christened him Elvis or Garth, but he always delivers. And now we have him bellowing out a ho-ho-ho instead. The things parents ask.

The snow is falling softly outside the window, right on Christmas cue. My wife wanted to host a Breakfast with Santa, so here we are with the neighbours in our townhouse complex, and the kids are decorating homemade gingerbread men, playing party games, and receiving a visit from Santa himself.

Tom, who's six, has told his parents that it won't be the real Santa. Not here, not in our living room. But after he climbs down from Santa's lap, he stops briefly, returns, and gives Santa a huge hug. Then returns to his parents and says, "He's the real Santa. I can tell."

Santa—the real Santa—has become the most politically incorrect character there is. An incongruous role model.

He's way overweight, he smokes a corn-cob pipe, he produces his toys in a remote offshore location using cheap, vertically challenged labour, he sneaks into people's houses in the middle of the night, little children happily sit on his knee even though they've been warned to beware of strangers, he drinks far too much Coca-Cola and he is in serious need of a haircut and shave.

What's he doing living in the North Pole anyway? Doesn't Mrs. Claus get bored up there? And cold? Isn't it a tad too harsh and isolated? Shouldn't Santa, who seems to be about 80 years old, be retired in Scottsdale or Florida? Do they play pinochle with the elves? Shuffleboard with the reindeer?

He may be giving up some of his vices. Almost two hundred years after Clement Moore gave us *The Night Before Christmas*, self-published Vancouver author Pamela McColl has excised the part where he has the stump of a pipe in his mouth and smoke encircles his head.

McColl says she wanted to update the book for the twenty-first century and remove the naughty part. I'd have kept the pipe and replaced the tobacco with medicinal marijuana.

Our modern-day Santa may be obese and merry and jolly—his cheeks like roses, his lips like a cherry—but as the writer David Sedaris observes, the European Saint Nicholas "is painfully thin and dresses not unlike the pope, topping his robes with a tall hat resembling an embroidered tea cozy." Santa has gone through updates and refinements over the centuries, and Coca-Cola in the 1930s gave us the version we have today.

But let's not try to change the old fellow too much, even as we all change and become more cynical and knowing.

He is a wonderful constant. Kind, magical, benevolent, and a testament to innocence.

Children around the world love him. And trust him. And much too soon they discover that it's not all magic and wonder out there.

The longer we can keep that innocence the better. Santa may not be perfect, may be increasingly politically incorrect (he even wears fur)—but let's not rush to fix his bad habits.

Merry Christmas, man. And to all a good night.

Let's talk about Santa, while we're here. In some parts of the world he's called Father Christmas, but he's obviously Grandfather Christmas. Look at the state of him. He's more than a little long in the tooth.

I mean, first, there's the weight thing. Jolly old elf? The man isn't just roly-poly; he's full-on obese. What kind of message is that to send to our children and grandchildren, many of whom are also mega-fat because they've spent too much time sitting in front of the tablets, smart phones, and gaming consoles Santa brought them last Christmas?

Santa should start nibbling on the carrots left for his reindeer, rather than tucking into mince pies, cookies, sherry, and such as he circles the globe. It takes eight—*eight!*—reindeer to pull the fat old fellow around the planet. They must be well and truly knackered by the time they've made it to the West Coast of North America.

So, a membership to a health club, Santa. We need a low-fat Santa. Santa in spandex. Then again, I've always railed against spandex on men of a certain age. Like, over forty. There's only so much body you can squeeze into activity-wear.

Then there's the big, long, white beard thing. What's he hiding under there? A multitude of chins? Nobody's worn long, shaggy beards since George Bernard Shaw. Any self-respecting beard-wearer (of which I'm one) knows that well-trimmed goatees are de rigueur nowadays.

He could do the day-old stubble thing, but that's a bit passé this week (you have to keep up).

Also, a dab of Grecian Formula wouldn't go awry. Santa might not have noticed, but old isn't hip at the moment. Well, old's hip, as long as you don't *look* old. Santa is of indeterminate age, but he's got to be the other side of eighty, and he doesn't exactly brim with youthful vitality.

That said, he *is* working—albeit one day a year. No Freedom 55 for Santa. I like that.

Okay, let's talk about the clothing. Not exactly *GQ*, is it, Santa? Santa, red is not the new black. Particularly white trim. Like, what kind of statement are you trying to make? Nobody, but nobody, wears red, except Team Canada (and a slew of other sports teams). And Santa, I can tell you're not into sports.

Okay, let's say you've never heard of Santa. You're from the moon. You walk around 2020 North America, and everyone is dressed in pretty drab, fairly uniform clothing. A little Gap here, some Eddie Bauer there, some Lululemon everywhere, and a whole bunch of khaki and knitted sweaters.

Then, suddenly, you see this very old man with a long beard walking down the street in a baggy—and very loud—red suit. No doubt you'd think, *well, this old fellow needs immediate medical attention. Or at least clothing advice.* Of course, being a Martian, you might be dressed in the same outfit, but the point is Santa's sartorially out of step.

Then there's the ho-ho-ho thing. Okay, this is a little personal, Santa, but no one these days clutches their little round belly—that has started to shake like a bowlful of jelly—and then, in a booming voice, goes: "Ho, ho, ho."

Look, Santa, this might be hard to take, but most of the world doesn't laugh much these days, and when it does it's with a restrained, almost cynical sneer. Irony is big. Sarcasm. Cruel humour. Not belly laughs.

And let's talk about the smoking and all that pipe-smoke encircling your head as you go into people's living rooms. First, you probably don't know this, but smoking is now fast becoming a crime punishable by public flogging. Smoking in someone's home—which you are apparently wont to do—will soon be a hanging offence.

And here's another thing, Santa. Not many houses have chimneys anymore. We all have fake gas fireplaces that look like real fireplaces because, well, we're idiots. So stop it with the clattering of tiny hooves on the roof already.

Plus, with property crime being what it is, are you sure you should still be sneaking into people's houses in the middle of the night?

And stop it with the "Happy Christmas to all and to all a good night" line—it's "Happy *holidays*," okay? Stop offending the non-Christians.

And finally, this stuff about making lists about who's been naughty and who's been nice, and then only rewarding the nice ones. Santa, what are you thinking? Those nasty kids are in need of help. We need to work with them. Not threaten them. You need to take a parenting course. Or a grandparenting course. This carrot-and-stick stuff is a little out of date. Plus, nice guys finish last. Trust me.

By next Christmas Eve, let's see a trimmed-down, non-smoking, non-chuckling, goatee-wearing Santa in a charcoal grey suit. That sounds like fun, doesn't it? Okay, maybe it doesn't. But Santa, we're just trying to help you fit into our ever-changing world.

Then again, he has given all grandfathers permission to be big and round and anti-social and concerned with making everyone around him very happy. And he has eyes that twinkle. So, yes, you're our hero too. •

Toys, Toys, Toys

Pow. Pow. Pzooooom. Pzeeeet.

"Ouch."

My grandchildren cornered me in the dining room and were all shooting me with laser guns. I wasn't sure how this game started with two teams of two and now it was three against one, but they were all standing in front of me, sending laser shots into the bullseye vest I was wearing.

"Not fair," I pleaded.

"Ha ha ha," they all replied enjoying their grandfather's suffering.

This set of four laser tag guns and vests came from Costco, and it was Linden's fourth birthday gift. He thought it was the best gift ever, though for some reason he thought he was supposed to bash me over the head with the rifle rather than staying ten paces away, as the house rules just established.

Now, I know this is a politically incorrect gift and is wrong on all kinds of levels, so shoot me. Every now and then, we fall short of our Boomer standards of peace and love and the whole thing because there's some fun to be had. And laser tag? Isn't that more *Star Wars* than *Deadwood*? And *Star Wars* is a Disney property now? Okay, best not to dwell. I'm uncomfortable defending myself.

When I was four years old, for my birthday, I received a Hopalong Cassidy cowboy set. It came with a hat, studded waistcoat, chaps, and a gun, and I was the envy of the street, where cowboy shootouts happened daily. We all had cap guns that were alarmingly loud.

Hopalong Cassidy was a movie and TV cowboy, played by William Boyd in the 1950s, and an unlikely hero for young kids. He was white-haired and wholesome and frankly looked more like a grandfather than a Clint Eastwood–style rugged cowboy. His drink of choice was sarsaparilla, a non-alcoholic tipple that never seemed to be available in postwar England. It sounded exotic and almost daring, even if the bad guys always laughed at Hopalong for favouring soft drinks rather than hard liquor.

My cowboy outfit had one flaw. The back of the waistcoat was made of tartan. After too briefly becoming the envy of the street, I was suddenly a figure of ridicule. Older kids started calling me McHopalong, and pointed and jeered at me, so the young cowboy ran home and cried to his mum and dad. My dad told me to tough it out

"Go and shoot them all, lad. That'll teach them." He had a wry smile on his face.

When our kids were young, guns had become a no-no. Some stores sold them, but parents shunned them. My brother-in-law Simon, believing the boys were being denied an important rite of passage, bought them both catapults. Not small, flimsy wooden catapults, but menacing, large metal catapults that, armed with a small rock, could put an eye out at a thousand paces. They were instantly confiscated, though the complaining continued for some time. Eventually we took the boys to the ocean's edge and let them fire rocks into the safe distance. No dolphins or flying fish were injured, so don't write in.

Emma and Linden are lucky to have a father—my son-in-law, Chris—who is basically a big kid. There isn't a toy he won't buy or build, and he gets more pleasure from the toy trucks or bouncy castles than his kids. Bouncy castle? Yes. He has one. Sorry, I mean, of course, the *kids* have one.

When Chris and Jani were first married, they had an impeccable townhouse with nary a thing out of place. Fast forward to today and two small children. Their living room is a chaos of toy trucks, toy drums, Lego, train tracks, balls, dolls, stuffies, garages, farms, and every delight a child could wish to play with.

Other kids come over for play dates just so they can go crazy in this toy shop of a house.

"I guess we're not very good at saying *no* to them," says Jani.

To be fair, Chris doesn't just use toys for their fun. He also creates houses out of cardboard boxes and once managed to make a slide out of cardboard that went from the top to the bottom of the stairs. Trying to descend the stairs on your feet without breaking your neck became a significant challenge.

Our grandkids play outside at every opportunity, and there's a playground at an adjacent park where they spend many hours swinging and sliding and climbing. And biking on the trails.

Emma and Linden mostly play with the same kind of toys, but Linden is addicted to trucks and cars and diggers. He also has a large new toy truck that is almost as big as my first car, a Renault Dauphine.

Our kids had their Cabbage Patch dolls, and our grandkids have their Elsas and Annas and Olafs, but what is heartening to watch is that though they have all the toys, they also have imagination. I see them using their toys to create small shows or magical scenarios.

Most important, for now, is they're not addicted to video games. I'm not so sure about their dad. •

9. Losing My Religion

"Do you believe in Jesus, Grandad?"

This was Emma speaking from the back of the car. We had been talking about Christmas and the nativity and the baby Jesus, and, sure being asked if you believe in Santa is one thing, but Jesus? Jesus!

I thought for a moment.

"I believe Jesus existed and that he was a good man, but I'm not sure if he was the son of God."

"Do you believe in God, then? Is *he* real, Grandad?"

We are now getting into tricky territory. My kids all went to Sunday school because we felt it was a good thing to do when they were young, but none of our grandkids have been anywhere near a church. Like a growing number of people in the Western world, religion is not at the heart—or even at the outer edges—of their world.

In reply to Emma, I told her many people believed there was a God, that there were many religions and beliefs, and she would have to work it out for herself.

"I'm still trying to work it out too," I said. "It's a big thing. Most importantly, you have to respect what other people believe in."

Thank goodness she didn't ask me about Santa.

I had another conversation with a then–nine-year-old Mayana about religion, or about the story of Christmas, and I was somewhat dumbfounded to realize she knew next to nothing about the Christmas story, the Magi, the shepherds, Bethlehem. She knew the baby Jesus was born in a stable, but there wasn't much more she could tell me.

And *there*, in a nutshell, is one of the biggest generational differences of all. Religion is not taught in public schools anymore. Not as a subject. It can be part of socials classes, comparative religions, and so on, but there's no central religious instruction.

As small kids growing up in the 1950s, we sang a hymn in assembly every morning. Usually "There Is a Green Hill Far Away." At high school, we were required to attend at least one class a week of RI—religious instruction—where the teacher talked us through some of the stuff in the Bible. I'm saying that's what she taught, but I'm not sure. I spent most of the time looking out the window, at green hills far away. And dreaming of soccer. One of the RI teachers could never keep control of his room, and the place was chaos. Rulers and erasers were thrown, kids jumped on desks, and he was routinely shouted down and ridiculed. I felt very sorry for him, even though I was never in his class, but heard the commotion next door. I'm not sure why he invited such bad behaviour, but maybe God was testing him, in some mysterious way. He never raised his voice at the students. I'd have thrown the Book at them. The heaviest one I could find.

Organized religion is going through a terrible time right now. When I go back to England, it's sad to see the majestic churches almost empty. Some have been deconsecrated and turned into homes or restaurants. Vicars now have to look after multiple churches and congregations.

Mayana's paternal grandparents are Sikh. My wife and I were brought up in the Church of England, but again, we're not into organized religion. We attended the United Church in Canada when our kids were in Sunday school, and later the Unitarian Church, which didn't seem to have one God, but accepted many. It was a place where we met many like-minded people, some of whom are still our friends. Once, at an anniversary dinner for our church, the crowd was asked, "Are there any draft dodgers here?"

About ten people stood up.

"And did anyone house a draft dodger?"

Just about everyone over the age of fifty stood up.

So my grandkids don't know how to sing "There Is a Green Hill Far Away," but they're good kids surrounded by good people and good thoughts. They're kind and gentle. Most of the time.

The one thing I should have told Emma, and I will, is that Jesus taught Love. Love your family, your neighbour, the poor, the helpless, the sick, even your enemies. Not exactly the Bible, but not a bad start. She and my other grandkids will have to work out the rest for themselves. •

10. I Need a Pee

What is it with small children and wanting to go for a pee *now*? "Now, Grandad! I can't wait!" I guess they all have tiny bladders, but they have an amazing facility for wanting to pee at the most inopportune moment. Usually in the middle of a traffic jam or in a movie theatre or when I'm up a ladder.

This past January we were in a Sidney thrift store when Linden beckoned me down and whispered into my ear.

"I really need to go, Grandad."

"Where?"

"Go pee." And then he started hopping from foot to foot in that time-honoured tradition of children down the ages. Linden was at this point barely four.

I picked him up and rushed to the counter, where the two assistants were in deep conversation with a customer. The conversation seemingly involved the entire history of the world or the mysteries of life itself, because there was no way they had noticed me or my grandson.

"*Excuse* me," I said with an air of desperation. "Is there a toilet in here?"

The assistants looked at each other, looked at me, at my grandson, and one of them, as though calculating his response, said. "No."

No?

"Really?" I asked, finding that hard to believe.

"Well, not for customers," said one of them, the younger of the two.

"It's for my *grandson*," I said pointing at Linden's angelic face. "He really needs to go. Can he use it?"

"No," said the older assistant. "They're not for customers."

There was a standoff for a few seconds. I put my grandson down.

"Linden," I said. "There is a toilet here, but you're not allowed to use it, so you're just going to have to pee here in the middle of this floor."

Linden looked at me with alarm, but not as much alarm as the shop assistants.

"Look," the young one sniffed, "there's a Starbucks just across the street, okay?"

For the sake of all of us I capitulated and took him there. Thank goodness for non-judgmental coffee shops.

Once, while I was driving along the M25, the nightmarish motorway that rings London, my granddaughter Emma announced from the back seat that she needed to go pee. Right now.

"There's a services area three miles ahead," I told Jani, who was sitting next to me.

"Too far," she said. "We have to stop."

So we did, on a hard shoulder, with nary a tree in sight, and Emma did her pee by the side of the car while passing drivers honked. In sympathy? They'd probably had to let their kids and grandkids pee on the motorway too.

The big new thing, while we're on the public lavatory issue, is the "nature pee." This is essentially going for a pee in the woods, by bushes, anywhere that's in nature. My three grandkids all do nature pees, even when there's very little nature around. A patch of grass, a tree, a hedge. Anywhere they can find something greenish.

I look the other way, whistle, act nonchalant. We've all gone pee in the woods. Thus far none have needed to water the neighbourhood daffodils (not yet anyway).

Of course, the need for nature pees at all only means that your leaky little cherub has graduated from diapers. A milestone to be celebrated because for all the convenience of the diaper years there is an obvious distasteful downside. Now I've changed my share of diapers over the years. With four kids and three grandkids—and one on the way—I have become something of an expert. A *reluctant* expert.

The thing is, I have a terribly weak stomach, and full and smelly diapers will have me heaving. Poop is not a pretty thing, so I have become practised at not actually *looking* at the contents of the diaper while doing the changing.

This was somewhat difficult when we used cloth diapers on our first born. I would somehow have to lie my daughter on a change table, or dining-room table—or wherever—lift her legs in the air and try to undo a safety pin, while looking at the ceiling and holding my breath. Then I would try to fold the diaper and its contents into a ball so I wouldn't have to look at it or inhale. And then I'd prick my finger on the safety pin. I don't like the sight of blood either, not when it's my blood.

I got better when we went onto disposable diapers, though I still often managed to put them on back to front. And then they'd be too baggy and leak, and let me tell you, a leaking diaper is something no grown man should have to see.

I'm better at it now. I still don't look or inhale, but I can now change a diaper blindfolded, which, let's face it, is by far the best way to do it. •

Okay Boomer

I think my generation is *supposed* to be offended by the "Okay Boomer" phrase. Depending on your view, it's either an attack on narrow-minded, outdated, condescending attitudes of older people, or an ironic, humourous slap at the generation that believes the world started and ended in the 1960s and no good has come of the world ever since.

It's somewhere between the two, I guess. We started the counter-culture thing. And now we're being laughed at.

I love it. Young people, particularly late teens and early twenty-somethings, are supposed to attack the status quo. They're supposed to tell the parents and grandparents that we screwed up. And we have screwed up. Many of us have nice homes, but our grandkids will have to live in shoeboxes. We didn't even know what climate change was—until we did of course. And so on. I could go on and on about what we did wrong, but why bother? Gen X and the Millennials have that covered.

But I *like* the Okay Boomer moniker.

It's about time my generation was laughed at and ridiculed on TikTok and Instagram and all those other platforms we don't quite understand but pretend to. The other night, I watched who won the main categories in the Grammys and was somewhat embarrassed—as a former rock critic—to realize that I knew barely any of the names of the performers in the main categories. I recognized many of the songs, but not the people. When I had last looked, Adele and Bruno Mars were huge, as were Taylor Swift and Drake and Ed Sheeran. They're still big, but all these newer performers came along to mess with my pop culture cred. Here was the Grammy headline on Yahoo the next day:

Billie Eilish's Sweep Leaves Li'l Room for Lil Nas X or Lizzo.

I confess I didn't know who they were, so had to go look them up and listened to them on YouTube. I kinda liked them. And instantly forgot them.

So be it. On the radio the other day I heard a DJ complaining that her mother had called Stormzy, the British hip-hop singer, "Onesy." Actually, that's not a bad name for a boomer-hip-hop artist. Onesy. It could be a new thing. Nobody would make fun of that. Right? •

Car Seats

I have mentioned this already. One of the biggest tests of being a modern grandfather is the kiddie car seat. It is the most baffling piece of engineering ever invented. There are harnesses and clips that defy logic, other straps that don't pull when they're supposed to and, worse, you somehow have to locate an anchor for the car seat somewhere between the back seat and the back rest. Your hand always gets stuck when you push it down inside.

Let's go back to our own childhoods. When we were kids, we bounced around in cars. We sat in the back of trucks. There was no such thing as a seatbelt. My first-ever ride, being cradled by my mother, was in a motorcycle sidecar. She was probably smoking too. It was a different age.

When our kids were young, they still bounced around, but we did have car seats for them in the back of our VW Westphalia. Sometimes they used them, often they didn't. The vehicle was spacious enough inside to play tag, or throw things at each other, which they did regularly.

And car seats were good places to put the smaller kids when *outside* the cars—when we had campfires on summer trips or even to strap them into canoes. We have a video of my wife and I paddling with our eldest daughter, Amy—then about ten months old—in Algonquin Park. She was strapped into her car seat and wearing a sun hat. Thank goodness we didn't tip.

Nowadays, most parents are religious about baby seats. Everything has to be tightened properly, anchored correctly, and facing backwards or forwards depending on age. The weight of the baby has to correlate with the seat. I think all this is a good thing. I'm all for protecting my grandkids, even if I do need a degree in engineering to figure it all out. But taking the seats in and out of the car every time we go to pick up the grandkids is a major pain. So I just leave the seats permanently anchored. If big people want to go back there, they'll just have to squeeze in between them.

All of which brings me to a huge difference between being a grandfather and a father. Your back.

In my pre-grandad days, I could happily carry my kids—front or back—in a pack up hills and down dales and, though I may be romanticizing this (you think?) I rarely if ever felt a twinge in my back. We went to a skating rink, and I helped do up their laces, before doing mine, and I bent over and held them upright as we skated around the rink.

We also went skiing. Somehow, we got them into their boots and carried their skis, and I helped teach them to ski while almost bending double. I held them as we went up T-bars and even rope tows, where I once burned my gloves clean through to the skin after half-holding the rope because a kid fell in front of us.

I gave them piggybacks, shoulder-carries, and swung them. I lifted them in and out of cars with ease and onto trampolines and all those other physical activities you didn't even think about.

Nowadays, and I'm somewhat embarrassed to admit this, I sometimes need help getting *my* skates on. Sometimes my back hurts so much I can barely bend over. Perhaps bending over too much and lifting up my own kids is a contributing factor. Or age.

Picking up your grandchild—lifting them off a swing or carrying them on your shoulders is still one of the most satisfying things you can do. But they get bigger and heavier real fast.

The other day Emma was on the stairs at her home when she called out for me to "Stay right there, Grandad!" before *leaping* into my arms.

I caught her. Put her down carefully. Then checked my back. So far, so good.

"My turn," said Linden.

Thank goodness he's a lot lighter than his sister. •

The Quiz

"Let's do a quiz, Grandad."

"Yes, yes, yes. A quiz!"

"Pleeeeease, Grandad. A quiz."

"Quiz. Quiz. Quiz."

Sometimes we sing in the car, like we did with our kids, but for some reason all three of my grandchildren love quizzes in the car. I become Alex Trebeck and ask each of them in turn a question.

These quizzes have helped get us through some very long car journeys. One, two or three of them—separately or together—want me to set questions on everything from animals to simple math or capitals of various countries.

The problem is, one child is now ten, one six, and the other four. One size does *not* fit all. So while I may ask Mayana the name of the president of the United States, and Emma the capital of Canada, I will ask Linden what sound a cow makes.

"Moo. Moo, Grandad."

"Brilliant. Pick up a Nobel Prize."

"What's a noble prize?"

I am actually a dab hand on animal noises. I can do all the basic farmyard animals and one or two more exotic wild creatures, such as bears, tigers, and lions (there's a subtle difference between a roar and a growl). I can also do squirrels and hyenas and an eagle, which has to have one of the most pathetic screeches of any of the big birds—such a sad tweet for such a majestic creature.

What I can't do, apparently, is imitate an elephant.

"What's this?" I asked one afternoon in the general round, where anyone can chime in, and then let out a loud *Phwheeeeeccchhhhhh …* or some such noise.

"What is *that?*" said Mayana, sounding disgusted. "It sounds awful."

"It's a cat that's dying," said Emma, who has a vivid imagination and will likely grow up to produce horror movies.

I did it again.

"An orca whale," guessed Mayana.

"A cow," said Linden.

"A slug that's been squished," said Emma.

"No, no, no," I said. "This might help."

And then, taking one arm off the steering wheel, I stuck my shoulder up to my nose and then let loose another majestic *Phweeeeeeeeechhh*—careful to keep my eyes on the road and other hand firmly on the wheel. Don't write in and complain.

All three children collapsed into giggles

"I know," said Mayana. "It's a dying seal with its tongue sticking out."

"No," I said, a bit offended. "It's an elephant."

A pause.

"Are you seriously telling us you're making the sound of an elephant?" asked Mayana incredulously.

"That's awful," agreed Emma.

"Is it still a cow?" asked Linden.

That was *so* an elephant, I started to tell them but then looked in the rear-view mirror to see all of them waving their arms, trunk-like in front of them, making *phwoor* and *phweeeee* and *moooo* noises.

I do find some comfort that the grandchildren are immensely entertained by quizzes, rather than burying their noses in an iPad, but before I get too holier-than-thou, there have been times on particularly long journeys when we've broken out a laptop and played a downloaded kids' movie.

The quizzes challenge me too. I have to work out questions on the fly that I think they have a fighting chance of answering, while moving between various subjects that might still entertain them.

And if I'm a second-rate elephant impersonator, so be it. I am a first-rate doofus, and sometimes that's all a grandfather has to be. •

Small Children Are Messy ———————————

Just before our grandkids come to stay, I take one last look around the living room and kitchen, where everything is "kind of" in order. Kind of. My wife and I are not neat freaks. We go for comfort ahead of style. Nobody's going to put our home in *Architectural Digest* magazine. Maybe in *Homes in Urgent Need of Renovation Monthly*.

But, you know, we can see the carpet. We can walk on the kitchen floor. We can sit at the dining room table and read a book without facing permanent injury.

One hour after the grandkids arrive, there is absolute chaos. Toy cars and Uno cards are strewn across the carpet, the kitchen floor is alive with popcorn and chocolate-flavoured cornflakes, the table is a minefield of books and unicorns and Lego pieces that dig into your funny bone once you make the mistake of leaning your elbow onto the table.

The chaos continues into the hall, up the stairs, onto the landing, and into various bedrooms, mine included because the bed makes the best trampoline, especially if you throw shirts and socks and many other soft and squishy things onto the mattress. And of course, there are the pillow fights, often instigated by my wife, who is frankly old enough to know better.

"Don't worry," she says as my grandson thwacks her with a pillow, sending stuffing spilling everywhere. "We'll put it all back together when they've gone home."

Ha!

We do have some friends who are neat and tidy people and whose homes you could put in magazines, but they exist just to make us feel inferior. Some of them even have grandchildren. I think they tie them up in the corner until it's time for them to go home again. I mean these people have figurines. I never see the point of figurines anyway, so we don't have any. My sister collects figurines of women in frilly dresses and puts them in glass cases. They provide her with much enjoyment, so who am I to quibble. Even if figurines are idiotic and belong in museums. The old kind of museums where nobody goes anymore. Because they're old. Any self-respecting museum these days has buttons to push and 3D glasses to wear and a nice coffee shop.

The writer P.J. O'Rourke put it best, in his book *The Bachelor Home Companion: A Practical Guide to Keeping House Like a Pig*:

> For toddlers, I suggest leaving their mittens on year-round, indoors and out. That way they can't get into aspirin bottles, liquor cabinets or boxes of kitchen matches. Also, it keeps their little hands clean for lunchtimes.

I only have one thing to add. When we had four young children in our house, and we were very much a lumpy, bumpy family, my wife found a magnet that she put on the fridge. It was from the poem "Song for a Fifth Child," by Ruth Hulbert Hamilton:

> *So quiet down, cobwebs. Dust, go to sleep.*
> *I'm rocking my baby. Babies don't keep.* •

Sleep Training

Speaking of babies and bedtimes, what has been fascinating to me, as a grandad three times over, is the very different parenting styles practised by our daughters. While Mayana, who lives on Salt Spring Island, is being brought up as a mini-hippy, Emma and Linden's upbringing has been much more conventional, in a nice three-bedroom house near Victoria.

When Emma arrived, for instance, her mum and dad employed sleep training. This meant she went to bed at exactly the same time each night, was put into a sleep sack, and a sound machine was turned on. This played meditative ocean sounds, and every time I sat in her bedroom with her, I too fell fast asleep.

The basic tenets of sleep training are that you introduce a sleep routine to the baby—from about six weeks old—so that they get into the habit of sleeping all night. The baby may get a bath, then a story, a lullaby, then they're popped into bed at a consistent bedtime. You then let your baby cry—for a time—go in and comfort them without picking them up and leave the room until they fall asleep.

Mayana, by contrast, went to bed at all kinds of hours—on weekends at least. It was, and is, still much more laissez-faire. Very modern and Mediterranean. I'm always impressed and a little appalled by those families in Italy or Spain who seem to start dining outside at around 8:00 p.m. with their entire family in tow. Mayana seems to go to bed when she feels like it, except on school nights when she is given a gentle suggestion that it might be a good time to go to bed. By this time, Emma and Linden would be well into dreamtime.

But both strategies seem to work well. They're all doing well at school, seem fit and happy and wide awake all the time, so who am I to quibble?

There's only one rule in our house. When they come to stay with us, they have to go to bed before I do. I do have some self-respect.

I have watched Emma grow from a tiny duckling into a swan of a young girl. Feisty, cheeky, artistic, and very funny.

And I have watched Linden grow from a happy baby into an adorable blond-haired young boy who loves cars and trucks and all the other stuff boys like. He's already melting hearts.

Emma and Linden's dad, Chris, is a super dad. He coaches them at soccer, builds and buys toys, and gives them endless adventures. Chris's parents, Barry and Jill, live in Lac La Hache in the BC Interior and adore their grandchildren as much as we do.

All my grandkids are out of central casting. Because they're my grandkids. Yours are too, I'd vouch. •

11. The Pier and the Charity Shop

There was a weekend this past January where we had all three grandkids. We had some good adventures, went five-pin bowling, ate pizza and popcorn in front of the movie *Peter Rabbit,* and played Sorry with Linden until, about halfway through, he got bored and went walkabout looking for his sister and cousin. My wife and I looked at one another.

"I guess it's game over," I said.

"Guess so." We quietly packed away the box.

Earlier that day, we had gone on a walk with our youngest son, Paul, Mayana, and Tucker the dog, and it had been wonderful. There were massive winds, and waves were crashing into the seawall and spray was flying over our heads. We got happily soaked and warmed up with coffees and hot chocolate.

But the real fun was on the Sunday. It was cold and rainy, and we had just dropped off Paul at the ferry. Now, with all three grandkids in tow and no dog, I said, "Let's go to the pier. It'll be cool."

What it *was* was freezing. The pier is really just a wooden fishing pier that juts into the sea. It's a hive of activity in summer. Not so much on a cold Sunday in January. But a few hardy souls had ventured outside and the wind had stopped blowing so hard. Rain still pierced our faces.

The three grandchildren skipped along the pier and, the fun part, started inventing games—skipping and running and squealing with delight. That's a thing we don't do as adults anymore. We just tramp along for the most part. Little kids run and jump and embrace the world. Then again, I'm not sure that if I ran jumping and squealing through the middle of downtown Vancouver at lunchtime that I'd be openly cheered by onlookers impressed by my youthful exuberance.

We got to the end of the pier, and a crab fisherman was pulling in his trap. He showed us his haul that morning, including one giant Dungeness crab and three smaller ones, all legal enough to eat.

We then watched a sailing race. About ten dinghies were zigzagging around buoys. "That one's stuck," said Emma. "Look, it's going backwards now."

Then I invented some races . . . ones where you had to walk on every board on the pier as you raced, looking like penguins, to the next bench. Then we had to run backwards. Then we had to hop on one foot. Then we found a wall and did obstacle races. Then seagulls swooped down to fight over some bait that had gone into the water, and three of the birds got into a major tug-of-war over a piece of squid.

"This is fun," said Mayana.

And it was. I am a pier fanatic. I grew up near the seaside in England, near a town called Southend, which boasted the longest pier in the world. The pier, more than a mile long, has over its history had musical halls, restaurants (Jamie Oliver opened one there), a bowling alley, amusement arcades and countless other attractions. And a train that still chugs from the esplanade to the "pier head." Like most piers built in Victorian times, it serves no useful purpose other than an amusing place to walk and take the sea air and people-watch others doing exactly the same thing.

The pier at Sidney is a modest but important part of the tradition. It kept us amused and the grandkids distracted for almost an hour. And it didn't cost us a dime.

The thrift shop down the street cost us a little more, once we got out of there, but it was money well spent. And, right here, I suggest that if you want to keep grandkids amused and you're at a loose end, head for a charity shop and watch them lose themselves in the toys, clothes, books, and other treasures. It is an adventure for you and for them.

While I was leafing through scores of books by Pierre Berton and Allan Fotheringham—so that's where they went—and more paperback thrillers than I could read in a lifetime, my grandkids were getting excited about every new, and inexpensive, discovery they'd just made.

When we exited, an hour later, we had spent $23.50. Most of that, $15, was spent by me on an ancient "electric slide viewer" that enables · me to go through hundreds of slides we took almost forty years ago. None of our projectors work anymore.

Emma bought earmuffs and a bag of small toys. Mayana bought soccer boots and a new sweatshirt. Linden bought a giant skateboarding action hero with bags of accessories that likely cost a hundred dollars when new, but he (or, rather, I) now acquired for six. Perfect recycling. And the treasures will likely be donated to another charity shop in a few months. Everyone wins.

It was an inexpensive half-day trip. One of imagination and good memories. And some good junk. •

Too Shy

So you're out with your grandchild, maybe in the local mall or in a park, and a friend comes by. You proudly introduce your grandson and granddaughter.

Nothing. They give you nothing. A blank stare.

Mayana and Emma were the worst when they were younger. They could be blithely chatting their heads off until mere moments before. But when introduced, they'd suddenly look at their feet and clam up. Or worse, they'd look right into the eyes of the stranger like deer caught in oncoming headlights.

"Say hello, Emma."

Nothing.

"Emma, just say hello,"

Silence.

"You know, she's not normally like this," I say.

"That's okay," the friend would say, "she's just a bit shy."

Linden is four years old, and he's perfected the silent treatment. He looks at the stranger, looks at me, looks at the sky for a second, then just gives everyone a big smile. Which, frankly, is a billion-dollar smile so he can get away with just about anything.

Of course, when they refuse to speak, I get more frustrated.

"Come on, Mayana, just say hello. Come on. Say hello. Say hello. Say hello."

To be fair, they seem to grow out of it. Mayana now chats amiably and—it makes my heart swell with pride—actually expounds on stuff.

"We just went to the toilet." That kind of thing.

You want them to perform, and they try to embarrass the heck out of you.

Emma once was painfully shy in front of those who weren't members of her immediate family and refused to perform on command. She'd dance this amazing ballet for us while I plonked on the piano. Then a friend would arrive, and I'd say, "Go on Emma, do what you just did."

And she'd leave the room.

For a while, as a toddler, Emma didn't like applause, so taking her to concerts was a challenge. One birthday we had to hum "Happy Birthday to You" because she would burst into tears if we sang too loud.

And then, suddenly, somebody turned on her chatty switch. Now she talks like an express train and will happily spill out her day, her week, her life story to anybody who asks. Or doesn't ask.

She likes to perform, to do little dances or major routines with Linden as her cute assistant, and she's adorable.

The other week, I took her into an English candy store in downtown Victoria. I told her to pick anything she wanted, as long as she didn't tell her parents and ate it before we got home.

I chatted for a few minutes with the shop owner about English candies, like aniseed balls, I used to eat as a youngster back in England. Eventually, Emma found the candy she wanted. And then told us that these candies had been in a goodie bag she'd received at a friend's party, and that there was a story behind them, because there was a TV character based on them, and . . ."

She didn't pause for breath. The store owner was attentive and supportive, listening in detail to this everlasting story. It was so long that two customers came into the store, looked around, checked out a few packages, and then left. I was afraid we had lost the store some business.

Emma was still talking. "Well, time to go," I said, thinking we could bankrupt this store if Emma went on much longer.

As we walked up the street, hand in hand, Emma looked up at me.

"You were a chatty Cathy in that shop, Grandad."

"Me?" I said. "I could hardly get a word in edgewise. You were the chatty Cathy."

"Well, you kept going on and on about old candy you liked. I just had to stand there and wait for you."

And then, she added, to punctuate the point, "You're a chatty Cathy. You're a chatty Cathy. You're . . ."

Like grandfather, like granddaughter.

Linden will emerge from his chrysalis of silence, I'm sure, but boys as we know are slower at these things. They still shuffle and look at their shoes when they're teenagers. And manage to look bored because you inflicted the outside world on them.

Linden is talking and singing and dancing to me already. Just for now, the audience can wait. •

Upside Down

One thing I can't figure out is why my granddaughters spend so much time upside down. They both go to gymnastics, and I've seen them at their classes, and they do bouncing and skipping and somersaults and such. But none of this explains why they're always standing on their hands and looking at the world upside down.

Linden doesn't do it. Well, he tries, but he just falls over.

Mayana started it. She'd been to acro-dance classes, a cross between acrobatics and dance, and from then on, I found myself talking to her feet as she stood on her hands.

Emma soon followed. When they weren't standing on their hands, they were doing impossible backflips and other contortions that were painful just to watch.

"Why do you keep doing that?" I once asked Mayana.

"Because it's fun, Grandad. You should try it." •

Riding a Bike

I taught all my four kids to ride a bike, running behind them and holding onto the saddle as they wobbled in front of me. The training wheels had been removed. And there was that moment of triumph when you could let go and they'd realize they could do it on their own, and off they'd fly.

My three grandkids can all ride a bike. All were helped enormously by those strider bikes, the ones that don't have pedals, and the kids just propel themselves around striding while riding.

It's still a magical moment when they get on a pedal bike and start on the adventure of a lifetime. I've loved riding bikes all my life and have ridden in London, Paris, Rome, and New York, as well as along the Danube, in Napa Valley, and across the Scottish Highlands.

But none compared to the moment when I rode with all three of my grandkids along a bike path near our home last year. My dream is to ride alongside them as long as I can, and as long as they still want to. •

Imagination

Imagination. I'm not sure how small children possess this amazing facility to venture into fantasylands and alternative realities without the use of hallucinogenic drugs.

Look at them playing with dolls, with small toy cars, or even a couple of blocks of wood. They go into a dreamland of adventures and dramas, zoom-zooming and having long conversations with nobody in particular.

Einstein said that imagination is more important than knowledge. Which is a good thing since I daydreamed through most of my chemistry, math, biology, and geography classes at high school. I missed many basic facts, such as algebra, trigonometry, the entire seventeenth-century history of Italy, and oxbow lakes, but I did score a lot of goals for Tottenham Hotspur in my head.

Imagination is important. It's the creative muse. And grandchildren seem to have the best imaginations of all. Linden will talk for hours about dinosaurs and purple elephants and how they went down into this cave and *phwoom phwoom*—his noise for a gun or a laser or some kind of neutralizing weapon that usually comes into play about two minutes into one of his stories. I think he's going to make action movies when he grows up. His movies will all contain trucks that blow up or crash into someone's kneecap.

Granddaughter Emma's stories are rich in imagery and short on detail, sort of like a lyric by Donovan. There are plenty of clouds, some fairies, woolly mammoths, and sometimes Elsa and Anna from *Frozen*.

When she was younger, Mayana used to assume a new identity, particularly for some obscure reason, when we went swimming at the local pool.

"Okay, Grandad. I'm Shirley and I'm going to swim to you because you're my swimming teacher." And then she'd be Shirley for the next hour or so, and I had to be called "Teacher" instead of "Grandad," and if I mistakenly called out something like "That was great swimming, Mayana," she'd glare at me and say, "Not Mayana . . . *Shirley*, Grandad."

"Surely you mean *Teacher*, Shirley."

Another glare, and then we were off into fantasyland some more.

For grandfathers there's an important lesson here. Our inclination is to limit rather than nurture imagination. Imagination, so I've learned, is an important tool for children to test out the world, try new ideas and situations. The grandfather, being more practical, will often try to correct his grandchildren and steer them towards logic and reality. Well, who the heck needs that when there's fun to be had?

More and more childhood educators are also telling us that we need to limit screen time, because it's killing imagination. Get the kids outdoors, playing games of imagination and wonder.

There's plenty of time to grow up. No need to rush things.

Thank goodness, however, Mayana didn't want me to be Shirley. •

Granddogs

I'm not sure what you call someone who's a grandparent of dogs. I do know that granddogs are, if not on a par with grandchildren, then one small step—or is that lope?—behind. And granddogs are certainly a thing. We who have granddogs know. They belong to our kids, so by association they belong to us—on weekends, on holidays, and sometimes for even longer periods. Free doggie-sitting.

Our granddogs are called Tucker and Bauer. And like grandchildren, they are adorable and needy and messy and know they can get away with just about anything when they are with us. Both are poorly trained, just like all grandchildren. And we try to lick them into shape, though they do most of the licking.

Tucker belongs to Amy, mother of Mayana, and has some English sheepdog, husky, some wolf and probably a few other attributes as well. His ancestors obviously slept around.

He is light brown with a small tuft of white hair on his chest and has a noble bearing. Other dog owners, when I take him to the doggie park, remark on how handsome he is, which makes me beam with pride. I'm not sure why. But he's a good dog to be with. I'm just happy he's not a Chihuahua or mini-poo or whatever they call those yappy little dogs that could fit into a purse.

Tucker has many qualities. Obedience is not one of them. In his first year of life, he'd run off as soon as he smelled deer or some other more interesting odour than us. Eventually he'd come back. Tail wagging, all covered in mud and other debris, with an almost apologetic look on his face.

"Bad dog," I'd say. "Never run away again." But he did.

He hated to be on a leash and would happily lunge at other dogs just about every time we took him for a walk. He didn't like to be constrained, or restrained, and would suddenly pull you halfway across the street as he tried to engage with a Doberman or a schnauzer or some such. Little dogs didn't seem to worry him as much, probably because he mistook them for dish towels.

He is in his element in the local doggie parks, where he can be off-leash and running. Tucker is fast and loves to "run" other dogs . . . meaning he will nudge them on the neck, run a few metres away, then challenge them to run after him. Most of them do. Some of the older dogs, whose running days are over, look at him, sigh and tell him to sod off, in doggy language. He gets the message and goes off to find a likelier running buddy, a greyhound or a German shepherd.

And then they run and run and run. In circles, in zigzags, as though possessed. They stop. Pant. And then run again. And then other dogs join them, and suddenly five or six dogs are running out of control, in absolute ecstasy.

Once in a while one of the older dogs will harrumph and decide, *what the hell*, and join in as their owners look on in amazement and tell me that they haven't seen their dogs run like this in years, watching their Timber or Charlie (modern-day dog owners pick very human names) careen towards a heart attack—like those geriatric joggers who waddle along on old bones and always seem to be on the verge of collapse.

Afterwards, I put Tucker on his leash, and we leave the park and he lunges at an Afghan hound.

Our other granddog is Bauer, owned by son Tim and his partner Jacy. He is their surrogate child. A Bernese mountain dog mixed with a little bit of Swiss mountain dog, which apparently makes him the most adorable dog on the planet.

When he was a puppy, I would sometimes take him out for a walk and every beautiful young woman en route wanted to stop and hug and kiss and pet him and tell him how adorable he was. Nobody ever did that to me. Even when I was a puppy. He still gets plenty of admiring comments and much patting and stroking when we go out, but he's a lot bigger now.

A *lot* bigger.

Bauer now weighs about 140 pounds, which is much heavier than my wife and only slightly lighter than me. Okay, me when I was nineteen years old—but I still live in hope and 33-inch khakis—32 inches on a good day. Okay, 34 inches.

Bauer bowls us over when he comes to stay, body going back and forth and tail wagging so rapidly that vases are knocked off side tables. Bauer bowls me over en route to my wife, who he adores. The feeling is pretty mutual. We don't have favourites, when it comes to kids and grandkids and granddogs, but apparently dogs do do—doo-doo?—favourites. Bauer loves his human mom and dad, but Beth makes him into a massive bowl of canine jelly, sloppy, wobbly, and if I may say so, rather soppy for a giant of a dog.

While Tucker is magnetically attracted to other dogs, Bauer has a cursory sniff of other dogs' butts and carries on along trails and roads, more interested in plants and sniffing territorial pee deposited by other dogs.

He is, however, attracted to water. Lakes, ponds, rivers, ocean—if it's wet, so is he. He rushes headlong into the water, splashing and swimming and creating liquid havoc. We keep him away from nesting birds in the spring, since dogs can apparently disrupt the delicate ecosystem that shore birds require. But Bauer is a one-dog ecological wrecking ball, so birds everywhere scatter when he's near.

The first time we doggie-sat Bauer, we took him for a walk along the seashore near our home. He gallumped and splashed around the water's edge, nuzzling stones and seaweed and was irresistibly cute.

Cute, that is, until three in the morning when I awoke and smelled something. I turned on the light and found doggie diarrhea on the carpet on the upstairs landing and all the way down the hall stairs. The smell was horrific, and I found myself gagging. Now, as you know, I've had my fill of diapers—four kids and three grandkids mean you have a pretty strong stomach—but doggie seaweedy diarrhea in the middle of the night is something I wouldn't wish on anyone, except maybe Donald Trump and that guy who cut me off on the highway this morning.

I cleaned and comforted Bauer as best I could, but he seemed fine. He'd done his business. The carpets needed professional cleaning. And Bauer seemed to learn his lesson—he has never eaten seaweed again.

Tucker and Bauer are an important part of our lives. We love them when they're with us. And we love them even more when we give them back. Just like—well, you know. •

12. Go, Red Team

My son-in-law, Chris, and I were watching the Superbowl. We were not huge football fans, but it was the Superbowl, and the grandkids were at swimming lessons, so it was the thing to do.

"You going for Kansas or San Francisco?" I asked.

"Kansas," he said. "They're the underdogs."

I told him I kinda like San Francisco but would have preferred Seattle or Green Bay. Man talk. I couldn't name one player on either team, but that's okay. I'm an older guy. I can fake things.

Then we watched the halftime show. Shakira and Jennifer Lopez. They are spectacular dancers and singers, and the show was over-the-top Americana at its best, and then Jennifer Lopez was, somehow, holding herself horizontal on a stripper's pole.

"That's very impressive," I said.

"Yes, and she's in her fifties."

"No," I said, and we checked online and she was exactly fifty.

"Crikey," I said. "I interviewed her once, at a movie junket in Los Angeles for the movie *U Turn*. The Oliver Stone movie." And then I realized that was more than twenty years ago.

I went into a reverie. She may be the only celebrity that I've actually interviewed who is still, so to speak, centre stage. Or centre stadium in this case. Over the years, I've interviewed many famous people, but at that precise moment I couldn't think of any who were still active. Or even alive. For some bizarre reason the only person who came to mind was Gregory Peck.

And then the kids arrived. Mayhem. Much leaping on the sofa on top of us and running around. Their hair was still wet from swimming.

Being modern guys, we had prepared dinner—a winter pot-pie I found in an old Moosewood recipe book, roast potatoes, and broccoli— and it would soon be ready.

"Who's winning?" asked Emma.

"It's a tie," said her dad.

"Come on, the red team," Emma said. "Go reds. Go reds. Go reds."

"Do you pick your favourite team because of the colour of their shirts?" I asked.

"Of course, Grandad." She looked at me as if I was crazy. "Red is the best colour."

"Why?"

"Because it's Canada's colour."

Suddenly I started supporting Kansas too. Red became a very attractive colour. Actually, when you think about it, that is just as legitimate reason as any to support a team. I have been to Kansas and San Francisco and like both cities, but I don't live there, have no particular attachment to either city, and frankly just wanted to see a good game.

When dinner was ready, we turned down the sound and ate our food and talked about the swimming and about a party they'd been to that morning, and my daughter asked about our recent weekend in Vancouver, talked about their upcoming holiday to Mexico, and suddenly the game had disappeared. Well, not totally. My son-in-law had been keeping an eye on things. When we'd all finished eating, he returned to his place in front of the TV.

"Four minutes to go. Exciting finish."

We piled onto the sofa again, and in an instant Kansas was in the lead. Emma, Linden, and I started doing football moves in the family room. They had to try and get by me before I could tackle them. This went on for quite a long time while Chris tried to watch the TV around us as we zigged and zagged and knocked over quite a few things.

Then the Kansas players dumped a tub of Gatorade over the coach. This, as sports fans will know, is an old tradition. The grandkids were stunned. They'd never seen grown men dump a whole bunch of energy drink over a much older man.

"Why'd they do that?" asked Emma in horror.

"Because they won. They're happy," said her dad.

"Is the old man crying?" asked Linden, quite concerned. "Did he know they were going to make him wet?"

Once we had reassured them that everything was fine, and that, yes, it was a very sticky drink, but the coach had a rain jacket so maybe he half-expected to be drenched, we put on the half-time show, which we'd recorded.

The show was mesmerizing. Both women wore next to nothing, and all the men seemed to be wearing baggy pants. "I want equal time," said my wife. "Why don't the men wear skimpy costumes?"

Jani was singing away to Shakira and Jennifer Lopez, and Linden was enjoying the fireworks onscreen, and though it was somewhat R-rated at times, with much bum wiggling and pelvis thrusting, we all agreed it was the best half-time show ever. At one point, after we'd been watching all the on-screen acrobatics, and maybe because I'd mentioned at least ten times that Jennifer Lopez was fifty, Beth said she'd read a piece in the newspaper that said if you could stand up from a cross-legged sitting position it proved you'd live a long time.

So Beth and Jani took turns trying to stand up without touching the ground with neither hands nor knees touching the ground. Jani did it. Beth almost. I had problems even sitting down cross-legged so abandoned the exercise.

"I interviewed Jennifer Lopez once," I bragged to Emma, seeking grandad cred. A pause. "Do you know who Jennifer Lopez is?"

"No," said Emma. "Can we watch that bit where they poured drink over that old man again?"

We did. The best Superbowl ever. I need to remind them not to pour energy drink over my head. •

Coaching Sports

On many Saturday mornings in winter, I can be found standing beside a soccer field yelling at my young granddaughters.

"Come on, Emma."

"Kick it, Mayana. Watch out, there's a player behind you."

Watching my granddaughters play soccer is one of the pleasures of my life, even though I usually do so in freezing cold or rainy weather since this is the West Coast of Canada in the dead of winter.

Sure, it's fun to watch them at a dance recital or singing at a Christmas concert or doing gymnastics, but soccer is what I did for fun when I was their age (though we called it football, being in England), and their mothers played it at their age, and now they're playing too.

The circle of life. Or kicking off of a tradition.

There are a few differences between the games I played then and they play now. The ball is certainly lighter these days and doesn't hurt your foot or, more crucially, your noggin when you kick or head it. Our balls were made of leather and for some reason attracted thick globs of mud like a magnet. Kicking a ball, which also became fossilized dead weight in cold weather, was excruciatingly painful. Today, thankfully, the ball is lighter, made of polyurethane or polyvinyl chloride, which you probably wouldn't want to eat, but won't hurt you if kicked. Our balls, just to punctuate the pain we had to endure, were stitched with laces. If those laces came into contact with your forehead, they would often leave a red mark, a tattoo of honour, sure, but your ears were still ringing minutes later.

I coached all four of my kids at soccer and enjoyed the experience. My favourite moment came while I was coaching Amy and her team, the Rainbows. (The girls picked the name. I had wanted the Sharks or something more aggressive, but I bowed to democracy.)

One Saturday morning we were playing on an all-weather pitch (essentially dirt and gravel) in a driving rainstorm. We coaches were urging the girls to run and run, though we'd all have rather been sitting warm and dry indoors, when the ball went into a puddle. At which point the girls on both teams, all aged about seven, ran to the edge of the puddle. And stopped.

"Get in there," I shouted.

"Get the ball," yelled the other coach.

At which point the girls looked at the ball, looked at each other, looked up at us, and resolutely refused to budge.

We yelled some more. Amy, to her credit, made a move to jump in the puddle, but thought better of it and looked at the other girls, and dared someone else to get it.

After a few more seconds of this, the referee, being about twelve years old, blew her whistle, shouted "drop ball," waded into the puddle and picked up the offending item, and carried it ten paces away onto a relatively dry surface.

Fast forward to 2015. Mayana was five years old and about to play her first game in a tournament with her new soccer team. My wife and I drove her to the field, and since we were running late, my wife ran with her onto the field while I parked the car.

About five minutes later, I got to the pitch in time for the warm-up to see my wife carrying Mayana and running a drill with the rest of the team. Up and down they went, in and out of some cones, and eventually the coach called in the girls for a pre-game pep talk.

"What happened?" I asked Beth.

"She got stage fright. She's scared. Most of the girls are bigger than her."

"Are you playing instead of her, then? Or just carrying her every time she goes on?

In the event, and tempted by the rumour of half-time team doughnuts, Mayana went on, played well and even scored a goal, even though it did appear to come off her knee when she was trying to avoid the ball. That didn't stop us punching the air and shouting "May-ana May-ana."

She now plays regularly, is no longer the smallest on the team, and scores goals with her feet. And I still cheer loudly, win, lose, or draw.

Linden isn't playing yet, not competitively, but he loves kicking a ball. Emma is in her second season playing, and it's cool to see her dad coaching her. She's quite the player for a six-year-old. I've already pencilled her in for a future Olympics.

Last year, she was a little less dynamic. One morning, before her game, I showed her a fancy soccer move, a la Cristiano Ronaldo who, if you aren't a soccer fan you should know has some of the best moves, dribbling and wiggling, in the soccer-playing world. The move had me wiggling one way, then the next, then running past the flummoxed defender and heading to goal to score.

"Practise with me," I said.

"Okay, Grandad."

And she wiggled and swivelled in front of me.

In the game, Emma—then aged five—had her father (the coach) and grandfather (the frustrated *former* coach) shouting sometimes contradictory instructions at her. I shut up after a while, mostly because of some glares from her dad. I was only trying to help.

Emma was playing defence. At one point, when the ball was at the other end of the pitch, I called to her. And did the Ronaldo swivel. Emma did it too. In fact she kept doing it, on the spot, as a player on the opposing team ran towards her, looked up in confusion at this young girl apparently trying to do the Twist, or similar dance in the middle of the game, ran around her and scored an easy goal.

After the game, she said, "Did you see my move, Grandad?"

And she did it again. A work in progress. •

Too Many Screens

Here's the biggest difference our lives and our grandchildren's lives: screens.

The only screen we were likely to see was a small black-and-white television. We watched it through squinty eyes and then we went out to play because, frankly, there wasn't too much to see there.

Our grandkids grow up in a world full of screens. Television, computers, tablets, mobile phones all playing *Frozen* and video games and music and other irresistible distractions. During my summer with Mayana, apart from the aforementioned TV moments, I tried to keep Mayana screen-free.

It was tough. Today it's part of a toddler's DNA. They already know their way around a mobile phone and where to find YouTube because it's always been there.

Not so long ago a survey by a British book company said that bedtime stories were dying out. Children, it claimed, have declining attention spans and are much more interested in on-screen activities.

They're spending at least four times as much time in front of a screen than reading. Scariest finding of all? Children today don't think reading is cool.

Some years ago, when I was a newspaper editor in Vancouver—before the Internet took over the planet—I introduced author Jim Trelease at a lecture called "What Turns Kids On to Reading."

Trelease, author of the bestseller *Read Aloud Handbook*, told the six hundred or so parents and teachers at the lecture that the best way to turn kids on to reading—and living—was to turn the TV off.

He asked us to consider what a child misses during the fifteen thousand hours (from birth to age seventeen) that he or she spends in front of the TV screen—and this was long *before* tablets and iPhones. The child is not working in the garage or garden with his parents. Not reading or collecting stamps . . . not listening to a discussion about community politics among his parents and their friends. Not playing baseball or going fishing or painting pictures. The screen is hijacking our kids' lives as they grow up.

Trelease didn't want us to ban television in our homes. That, he says, would be elitist. Television, used properly and rationed effectively, can be a valuable medium, and I concur. Most of us, however, are prime-time TVholics. Game shows, sitcoms, reality shows, soaps, and other such pap form our steady diet. When was the last time you watched anything on PBS?

Some of Trelease's points:

Television is the direct opposite of reading. In breaking its programs into eight-minute commercial segments, it requires and fosters a short attention span. Good children's books hold children's attention, they don't interrupt it.

Television is relentless: no time is allowed to ponder characters' thoughts or recall their words because the images move too quickly. Books, meanwhile, encourage a critical reaction. The reader moves at his or her own pace, able to pause to ponder meaning.

Television deprives the child of their most important learning tool—questions. Children learn most by questioning. For the thirty-three hours a week the average kindergartner watches television, they can neither ask a question nor receive an answer.

Television desensitizes the child. Extensive research over the ten years prior to Trelease's lecture had shown TV's bombardment of violent images (eighteen thousand acts viewed between the ages of three and seventeen) makes the child insensitive to violence and its victims—most of whom the child believes die cleanly or crawl inconsequentially offstage. Yes, says Trelease, literature can also be violent. But one researcher showed you would have to read all thirty-seven of Shakespeare's plays in order to experience the same number of acts of human violence (fifty-four) that you would see in just three evenings of prime-time TV.

Trelease's message was to read to your kids. Spend time with them. Enjoy them.

The larger message, however, was for all of us. The less we watch others doing, the more we do ourselves, the more we think for ourselves, the better our world becomes.

The screen—*every* screen—is a great way to keep your child or grandchild amused. It's also a good way for them to become desensitized, out of shape, lazy.

So go out and throw a ball with your granddaughter. Make some cookies with your grandson.

Or best of all, read them a bedtime story. You're the best hope they have. •

Playing Dress-up

When you get to my age and you have all the offspring I have, you have attended your fair share of school concerts, shows, and Christmas spectaculars. I think some kind of medal is in order.

My kids appeared in myriad shows. Amy was Dorothy in *The Wizard of Oz*. Jani was Alice in *Alice in Wonderland*. Tim pretended to play trumpet in the school band. (He hated the trumpet but wanted to go on a school trip, so mimed perfectly and got to go. I give him marks for creativity, if not musicianship.) And Paul has played a rose, Santa, and a news anchor, which is his current gig—he gets paid for that one.

And now it's my turn to watch my grandkids. Mayana has sung and danced in many concerts and most recently acted in a school show in which she had to play a reporter. My buttons popped with pride right there.

Recently, I was sitting in a gymnasium watching Emma as a rabbit. She was playing Cottontail in the kindergarten production of *Peter Rabbit*, and she was wearing cute ears and waving at us. She looked confident, eager, and happy.

This is a minor miracle. Emma, before she attended school, got terrible stage fright, even in the living room. Once, famously, she had a meltdown just before a school concert and refused to go on. Her parents—dressed in their finest and with cameras ready—spent the entire concert hugging their daughter backstage.

Emma developed amazing confidence and will now put on shows for the family, turning cartwheels and dancing around while younger brother Linden tries to keep up, usually falls over a lot, and then bows proudly at the end.

There is a system to the school concert. Kindergarten children are not there to do much except look cute. They wave at their parents, appear confused, generally ignore the teacher, wave some more, and then look around the hall in a glazed, absent-minded way, likely thinking, *is my dad filming this and will he embarrass me in twenty-five years' time by playing clips at my wedding so that everyone can laugh at me again? Will this hell never end? I know, I'll wave some more. And scratch my bum.*

Older kids have practised a song that they will sing out of tune, if they remember the words, and try to look as startled as possible, especially the boys who will not sing but stare defiantly ahead (except for little Johnny, who is teacher's pet and always behaves impeccably).

Things improve but become a whole lot less cute as the kids get older. The parents are still besotted and watch only their child—even if their child is in the back row and hidden from view. Older children do not wave, but their parents do, much to their child's embarrassment. So while their teacher is pleading with them to smile, they are instead lost in an embarrassed scowl. Thinking, *will this hell never end?*

Some concerts do last, well, forever as each class troops out to do its party piece. Sorry, I may be a little jaded. But, yes, they *can* be magical. Emma sang with her class at a school Remembrance Day concert recently, holding onto a small poppy. And she looked cherubic. And the song broke your heart. And there wasn't a dry eye in the house.

It's strange, when you think about it—how we dress up our kids and grandkids and ask them to perform for us. Even if they don't want to.

And while we're on the subject of dressing up kids, when did young girls become such fashionistas? Not the boys. Linden is happy in anything and will wear his pyjamas all day if you let him. Sort of like his grandad then.

Mayana and Emma, however, have always been very conscious about what they wear. Mayana likes to wear cool ankle boots, Bolero-style hats, and smart jackets and sports a kind of Salt Spring chic, some second-hand, some new, and she always looks good.

Emma, meanwhile, wears waistcoats, vivid shirts, and special multi-coloured tights called Sweet Legs. I asked her why they were called Sweet Legs. She looked at me as though I was crazy. "Because they're sweet, Grandad."

Duh.

We have a dress-up box—an old trunk—and the kids spend hours digging in there. Linden will emerge with funny hats and clown masks, and Emma will find an old Halloween bear costume, or a leopard outfit, and she will wear it all day, and even to bed that night. And yes, little children still like to put on their parents' high-heel shoes and clunk around, pretending to be grownups.

I think old-style grandparents used to worry and fuss about what their grandkids wore when they went out with them. Nowadays wearing a tutu on the high street is just fine. Boy or girl.

Emma's latest thing is to wear ankle boots to the beach, which makes a change from sandals, I guess. Though she did invent the sand-sock, in which she wades into the ocean up to her ankles, then buries her feet in soft sand, which sticks to her ankles as she parades up and down in a kind of kiddie-catwalk.

I bought Emma and Mayana dresses when I was in Spain a couple of years ago. Mayana loved hers—a nautical design with red and blue horizontal stripes—while Emma seemed somewhat less enthusiastic. I asked her about it later.

"It was nice, Grandad," she said carefully, trying not to hurt my feelings, "but I didn't like that frilly bit around the hem. If the frilly bit had been higher, maybe, just under the waist, it would have been much better."

Perhaps I looked crestfallen because she added, "I know, Grandad, we can cut the frilly bit off. Then it'll be more grownup."

Just like Emma. •

13. New Normals

The phone buzzed. My wife picked it up, looked at the screen, and started squealing—with joy, as it turns out, though she had me worried.

"Emma, it's fantastic! Look at you. Does it hurt?"

Mystified, I lean in and look at the screen, where Emma is on FaceTime showing she just lost a front tooth. It has been wiggling for weeks and it has finally come out. She looks like a hockey player.

A grandchild. A lost tooth. This is a *big* deal.

There is much discussion about tooth fairies and how much money they leave these days. Three dollars seems to be the going rate, though on our family WhatsApp site later that day my older kids say the most they ever got was twenty-five cents. One child says he found five dollars when his teeth came out when he was camping, but figures it dropped out of his dad's pocket in the tent by mistake.

This is how many families communicate these days—virtually and immediately—and during the early days of the COVID-19 crisis, it was the only way we could see our grandchildren up close and personal. On FaceTime, Skype, Google Hangouts, Zoom, WhatsApp, Facebook and myriad other platforms, including the good old telephone, we shared our experiences and our joys and fears and tears.

COVID-19 and early lockdowns around the world were a challenging time for everyone, but especially for older grandparents trapped in care homes where visits of any kind were banned. For us, it wasn't so bad, even though, at first, we didn't get to see our three grandkids at all because of social distancing.

Worse, we couldn't help out with babysitting. My son-in-law worked from home with two young children bouncing around the house. He showed an amazing calm throughout. I remember working from home many years ago as a newspaper correspondent with four kids around, and it had many stressful moments. Once I was interviewing a former prime minister by phone when my then–six-year-old son Paul rushed into my office.

"Dad, I can't find my socks."

I put the phone down quietly, rushed out to his bedroom, and found two socks that almost matched and then rushed back to the phone to hear the prime minister complete a very long answer. I still wonder what I might have missed in those twenty seconds. A stunning national revelation, or confession, missed because of a pair of socks.

After the early days of COVID-19 lockdown, we began to edge ever closer to the grandchildren. We kayaked to a beach on Salt Spring and had a socially distanced picnic with Amy and Mayana.

And we had two picnics on quiet beaches nearer to home with our daughter and smaller grandkids. Emma and Linden were amazing, keeping a distance from us, never breaking the invisible barrier. They seemed to be better at it than their grandparents.

COVID-19 has recalibrated most of our lives for many years to come, but it also showed me the resilience of small children. They seemed to get on with their lives with a confidence and optimism and a collective shrug. *So what?* they seemed to say. *We've got this.* Sure, they missed school. They missed friends. But most of the kids I saw seemed to go about their lives as if everything would turn out fine tomorrow. And the next day.

Around them there were daily box scores of numbers of infected and dead, and they saw everything about them shut down, and they heard new expressions such as "flatten the curve" and "keep your distance." But they were also told to wash their hands a lot, which was nothing new to a four-year-old.

We celebrated two family birthdays and Mother's Day with multi-screen get-togethers in the early days of COVID-19, though I noticed all three grandkids got bored after a few minutes and went off screen to look for food or do somersaults or read a book or play with a toy. The virtual get-togethers were pretty successful. I also did a bunch of work meetings virtually—and that will likely be the new normal. I can't believe I used to fly from Vancouver to Toronto, sometimes three times a month, to attend meetings. That now seems wrong on so many levels. It seems even the *recent* past is another country.

COVID-19 purportedly made most of us kinder, and I think that's true. And more reflective. And it made us consider what's important. While the world was on hold, we had a little more time to think, to consider who we are. There were many awful downsides to the worldwide pandemic, but many positives too.

The world certainly learned about the fragility and vulnerability of their parents and grandparents. We learned not to take older people for granted. I was moved when I watched a BBC documentary that profiled some older people who had died of COVID-19 in care homes. It showed that they were not old wrinklies, a stereotype of doddering inanity, but had been heroes and veterans and had done remarkable things They were musicians and teachers and Second World War prisoners, and suddenly they were real and not a statistic.

Our own children aren't taking us so much for granted either. The joke, in the early days of the crisis, was that once we told our children not to stay out—and now they were telling us to stay home. Many people in their sixties said they had been hectored and lectured by their children and told to be careful. As my own son put it . . .

"We'd like you around a little longer, please."

The world has been changed by COVID-19, and new normal is the new mantra. But the subtext is it will never be the old normal again. We are all of us—including our grandchildren—facing a different world than we had before. With luck it will be a simpler, kinder world. One our grandchildren will inhabit with relish.

We have all learned a lot. About the world and ourselves.

For one thing, we figured out that air-hugs and high-fives and blowing kisses from a distance can still work. Kinda. And my grandson also figured out that a garden hose can still hit his grandfather from a distance of more than two metres—and then saying, "Oops, sorry, Grandad, I made a mistake," can still melt your heart, if accompanied by a cheeky grin. •

14. Past, Present, and Future

One of my favourite quotes comes from twentieth-century British novelist L.P. Hartley:

The past is another country; they do things differently there.

That's certainly true when it comes to today's grandchildren. Our past is mostly a mystery to them, another time and place, another world. You mean they didn't have smartphones, Grandad? No Netflix? How did you survive?

My past is still very much with me, and every now and then I remember a very happy time from my childhood. We can never quite escape who we were. Sometimes I'd like to go have a chat with my younger self and give him some sage advice. Don't smoke. Try and stop dressing like a slob. Don't watch so much schlock TV. And go and buy stock in something called Microsoft before anyone else does. In fact, go and make friends with a kid called Bill Gates. I probably wouldn't listen to myself, or the smarter side of myself. Never did, likely never will.

We may look fondly at the past, to the fifties and sixties, but we gloss over the rampant racism, homophobia, discrimination, sexism, abuse, and cruelty that were also part of the fabric of the age. Sure, many of us had the summer of love, but we sure had many summers and winters of hate.

We look through the past with rose-tinted glasses. I loved my childhood, in a small town near the seaside in England. I loved being a kid. And a teenager. Playing and laughing and being part of a large loving family, even if my mother and her siblings sure seemed to fight a lot—or *fall out*, as they put it, which meant they stopped talking to one another for a time because someone looked at someone else funny, or said something, or didn't say something. I could never quite keep up. They were from Yorkshire. Maybe it went, literally, with the territory.

I also loved TV comedy, everything from *The Dick Van Dyke Show* to a British sitcom called *The Likely Lads*. One of my two favourites were *Doctor in the House* and *On the Buses*. As a young reporter who enjoyed writing about entertainment, I interviewed many of the cast members of both shows.

Some years ago, a colleague at the TV station where I worked in Canada told me he had many of those old British sitcoms on video tape. Would I like to borrow them for a weekend? Would I!

My kids were then pretty young, but I *knew* they'd find them hilarious too, so I parked all the kids in front of the TV and put in the cassette tape. The first show was an episode of *On the Buses*.

"I was a bus conductor when I was a student," I told them, "and some of the scenes were filmed at my old bus garage. And that woman there, Olive, I interviewed her too. She looks frumpy and boring, but she was actually quite glamorous and needed lots of makeup and . . ."

And I realized nobody was laughing. And I wasn't laughing either. There wasn't anything remotely funny happening and, worse, one of the characters seemed to be doing nothing but haranguing poor old Olive and calling her a daft old bat or an ugly old cow.

So we stopped watching that show and put on *Doctor in the House*. I had interviewed Barry Evans, the star. He was funny, cute, short, and adorable. My role model, though I never told my kids that. I wanted them to see it for themselves.

But again, no laughter. I found myself cringing too.

"Maybe that was just a bad one," I said, and put in another episode.

It was worse. We turned it off.

"Sorry kids," I said. "It seemed funnier at the time."

The fact is, much of comedy doesn't age well. Look at *The Honeymooners* and Jackie Gleason threatening to send Audrey

Meadows "to the moon." It's one of the most memorable TV lines of all time, but the idea of hitting your wife so hard she'd go into orbit doesn't seem so funny anymore. Or ever.

We used to watch *The Cosby Show* with our kids. And now we want to erase that from our memories quickly. My kids won't be showing their kids old tapes of that one, now that Cosby has been shown to be the opposite of the kindly father and grandfather we all thought he was.

Yes, the past is literally and metaphorically another country for me, as I've noted before. Very nice . . . but I don't want to live there, not in the past. There is, as the old song goes, still a lot of living to do.

Okay, as the French kind of say, Past Imperfect, Present Tense, and Future Conditional. Let's get to the present. To the now.

The Buddhists and those who practise mindfulness probably have it right when they urge us to live in the present. To be aware and in the moment rather than living in the past or worrying too much about the future. Which reminds me of another favourite quote, at Christmas:

"You can't change the past. You can't predict the future. And there are no presents."

But as we become older, we do have a tendency to live in yesterday. Mostly because the music was better. And, perhaps, so were we.

We do have an urge to tell our grandchildren where we, and by extension, they came from. What our world was like. Even if, right now, as preteens, they don't care.

I want to tell them about a world before computers and colour television, a world where you were lucky to go to a restaurant once a year, where you read books for fun, where you rode just about everywhere on a bike or a bus because you were lucky if your family had a car.

And then that dreaded phrase: "When I was your age . . ."

And the glazing over of young eyes. Sure, Grandpa, you lived in a box and walked barefoot in snow in both directions to get to school where they beat you because you were too hungry to keep your eyes open.

Okay, not that bad. But I get the drift. More fun to stay in the present, a world in which we both live and can relate. Where the past doesn't seem as important anymore. And, sure, if I can drop in the odd war story, or traipse down memory lane when they're in the mood, then that's fine.

They do enjoy looking at old photo albums, mostly to see what their mums and dads looked like when they were younger. We also shot plenty of Super 8 video when they were young, and, now digitized, can be fun to watch on a winter's day. Especially the one in which all of our kids—their parents—did a Christmas show in the living room. It makes me laugh and wipe away a tear every time I watch it. I hope my grandkids will watch it well into the next century.

COVID-19 aside, the present is, right now, a wonderful time. Partly because I'm a grandfather. The thing, as you get older, is still to find a purpose, a reason to be. Being a grandfather is a large part of that. But not the only part. Living for today, smelling the roses, and appreciating the world around you, is frankly a lot easier as you get older. You don't have a lot more to prove, people to impress. You are who you are. And because you've lived longer than you're going to live, and because your own future is uncertain, you tend to treasure every minute you have. I'm not sure why grumpy old men get that way. Regret? Lost youth? Frustration that all the bits of your body don't work as well as they used to? Perhaps.

So the past is taken care of, the present is fine, but what of the future.

I do worry sometimes about the kind of world we've left our grandchildren. Just the other day I saw a documentary that predicted the world's population, now hovering around 7.7 billion, will be 10 billion by 2050. There will be huge challenges in terms of food and water. And if the rest of the world were to consume at the rate of North Americans, we'll be lucky to get out of this century without major catastrophic events.

Okay, let's get this out of the way. Grandparents, most of us Boomers, have to wear some guilt and shame for leaving our grandkids a very imperfect future. We were going to make it a better world. Sure, in many ways it is. Racism and discrimination and homophobia and sexism are still with us, but now we are confronting it. We can do better. Sure. But I'm an optimist, and I figure things can and will improve if we have the will.

The world is still on edge. We mistrust our leaders. And our sense of place has forever changed. There's so much noise and chaos right now, that trying to make sense of it all gives you a permanent headache.

I am worried and excited about the future and the world our grandchildren will inherit. We have to do a lot more about climate change, sure, and stop using plastics. (How strange in *The Graduate* that Mr. Robinson tells Benjamin to remember one word. Plastics! That's where he'll make his fortune. No wonder Mrs. Robinson decided to go rumpy-pumpy with Benjamin. She knew her husband was a limp climate denier.)

Our Boomer generation has consumed until we're blue in the face, as the planet becomes less blue and more grey. We flew and drove everywhere we could and kept our light bulbs burning when we didn't need them.

And, yes, even after COVID-19 and how we learned a virus can wreak havoc around the world, I have faith in the future. In our kids and grandkids, who seem now to be a lot smarter and aware than we were. Even our generation is getting a lot better at everything from recycling and using public transit and eating locally. It's a journey.

I haven't got much time for climate change deniers. But our communities and more and more businesses are waking up. We're seeing the demise of the plastic bag and increasing pressure on companies to use less packaging. In our own house we put out very little garbage these days—but recycle plenty. I called my wife St. Beth of the Environment thirty years ago, and because of her we've largely walked the talk. I'm still lousy at the plastic bag thing because we have a bunch of recyclable bags, but I always forget them.

"I'm fine," I say at the supermarket checkout. "I don't need a bag, I'll juggle." And then I head to the parking lot with bananas, grapefruit, cereal and assorted cans and then, somehow, have to locate my car key without sending everything dropping on the ground. I did lose three oranges once, under a large truck. I figured they'd decompose eventually.

The future, technologically, looks amazing. And scary as hell. The century in which we grandfathers were born saw the most rapid technological change in our planet's history. At the beginning of the twentieth century, Wilbur and Orville Wright were trying to get their powered rudimentary plane into the air. By its end we had been to the moon and back a few times, flights around the world became routine, and this thing called a computer radically shifted every paradigm in the book.

On the way, it destroyed countless newspapers—my means of employment for many years—and many other industries. But technology, and some gifted individuals, helped us live longer and healthier and made the world infinitely more interesting. In the twentieth century we all got to live like royalty. We saw more places, we got entertained by more things than the nobility of olden days, and though, as the writer Neil Postman once posited, we entertained ourselves to death, well, it was quite the ride.

We can't even begin to predict the world in which our grand-children will be adults. At the beginning of the last century, mail in America was delivered by stagecoach. The head of Wells Fargo at the time predicted that's how mail would be delivered by the end of the century. Sure, he had a vested interest, but we can forgive his lack of vision. Nobody back then could predict email, Instagram, Facebook, TikTok, or the many other ways of communicating. Today the telephone is hardly just that anymore. It opens a world of wonder every time we take it out of our pockets.

And the rate of change is head-spinning. Look at music and television. We have, in our lifetimes, seen not only the demise of the 45 and 33⅓ rpm record, but also the introduction of the eight-track and compact disc, and then their replacement by streaming services. The video stores came with their VHS and Beta, and then DVD, and now Blockbuster is no more, and we have Netflix and Apple TV and count-less other ways to get our movie fix.

How far can technology now go? I'd say, *to the moon, Alice,* but it's already taken us there. But not, thankfully, Alice.

I once did a project for a media company predicting what the future of newspapers would look like. As part of that project our group spoke to some of the super-brains at the Massachusetts Institute of Technology. They almost predicted the future of electronic newspapers, though they didn't at that time predict cellular or WiFi access. They saw us taking a tablet—this was way before iPads had been invented—to a corner box owned by the newspaper. We would stick it into a slot, and the latest news would be downloaded.

Wow, we all said, and went home to cut down a bunch of trees and turn them into newsprint because we figured most of our readers would prefer their news to be given to them. Ah, what stupid innocents we were. In our defence, we pointed out in our final report that we were no longer in the newspaper business, but the news and "content" business—and had to give our readers the news on any platform they preferred. Well, at least we got that part right.

But one of those MIT super-brains told us something that hasn't quite happened. Yet. We could, he said, one day have microchips inserted into our heads and we could, just by thinking, dial up any TV show, or book, or newspaper, or movie on a virtual screen in front of us.

Whoa. Big Brother looms, we all said. And yet, Alexa and Google Play and Facebook et al are already reading our preferences, our minds, our algorithms. I wouldn't be shocked if that virtual screen doesn't catch on. If I'm still here I'll have a 65-inch wraparound in 3D, please.

I have read some books of late predicting what the world will look like by the end of the twenty-first century. We will have hover cars, driven by compressed power. Oil won't exist. We will live in smart homes that can predict our needs and even monitor our health.

"Mr. Smith," says the virtual future Alexa, "we have detected a minor tumour growing on your left kneecap. We have scheduled an operation next Tuesday."

Scientists say we can't even begin to predict this future. But it promises to be a wild ride. With upsides and downsides. We will have toothbrushes that can clean our teeth with sonar in ten seconds. But will we have a brain, to paraphrase the scarecrow in *The Wizard of Oz*? Artificial Intelligence, like the robots before them, will eliminate more and more jobs—but will they also eliminate our need to think, to analyze, to reason, to be? The future is exciting. And perhaps Orwellian.

I wish my grandkids lots of luck. I wish I could be there with them. •

Other Grandfathers

I must confess that I was a reluctant grandparent at first.

In a youth-obsessed society, where every wrinkle is a badge of shame, being a grandparent isn't exactly something you shout from the rooftops. "Hey, grandpa" can be an insult in the workplace. It means you're past it, old timer. Go sit in your rocking chair.

And yet.

Mick Jagger, wrinkles and all, is a great-grandfather.

Roger Daltrey of The Who, who once sang that he hoped he'd die before he got old, is a grandpa at least ten times over.

Paul McCartney is a proud grandad, as is Ringo. McCartney even wrote a kids' picture book, *Hey Grandude!* in which the grandfather is, yes, a cool dude who goes on adventures with his grandkids.

Jim Carrey. Tom Hanks. Steven Tyler of Aerosmith. Kiefer Sutherland. Pierce Brosnan. Harrison Ford. All grandfathers. Daltrey has taken the grandfather role very seriously. He recorded a version of "The Wheels on the Bus" for toddlers. No guitars were smashed in the recording.

Bob Dylan has several grandchildren, and though nobody can understand a word he's singing these days, he still manages to fill concert halls around the world. One of his grandsons, Pablo, is a rapper, and calls Dylan "the Jay-Z of his time," which would mean something cool and hip and life affirming to every grandfather on the planet, if only we knew who Jay-Z is. Or could at least hum one of his songs.

The thing is, being a grandfather isn't a stereotype any more. Or we hope it isn't. We are not our grandfathers—we are very much a new breed. But there is one common thread. We're proud to be grandpas and granddads, and we like to tell stories—to our grandkids, and about them.

As part of this book, I thought it would be cool to ask some of my friends—grandfathers, and in one case, a granddaughter—to write something about grandparenting. I'm grateful to them for their contributions. Because it's not all about me. At least not all the time.

Enjoy. •

Donald MacGregor

Donald is a doctor in Perth, Scotland. He and his family are great outdoors people, hiking and biking up and down mountain and dale. He's a great friend and a super grandad.

I have three grandchildren: Ava (seven), Ben (five), and Gregor (two). I have said from early in my grandparenting career that even just five minutes with Ava (and same holds for her siblings) puts a smile on my face for the rest of the day—a great prescription for life. But now Ava is older she's a wee bit suspicious that Grandpa is smiling/laughing *at* rather than *with* her ... maybe true at times. I suspect Ian has had some of the same with Mayana, as I remember her mum (Amy) as a wee girl bursting full of life and ideas who brought light and fun with her.

My grandchildren know Ian well, having had to wait for him many times on a cycle trip through Scotland's Highlands this year! They are kind—like their grandpa. Having said that it is *very* difficult to relate stories about your own grandchildren without it being a "grandpa boast"...this is acceptable ... well, it is is for *my* grandchildren

I am a pediatrician, and my wife, Elspeth, a children's public health nurse, but when No. 1 grandchild was to be placed in our care she came with a *long* list of instructions/contact information and regular reminders to update on progress (some of which we managed!), No. 2 grandchild with an occasional text or WhatsApp and No, 3 ... "don't call us, we'll call you!"

As a "cool" Grandpa, I always wanted to give them great fun and adventures and in spite of best efforts I often returned "damaged goods," them having fallen off logs crossing streams, swingpark tumbles, or just simple trips etc. and necessitating a trip to the local drug store to get sticking plasters, Arnica (anti-bruise cream). And the assistants seemed immediately wise to the situation and anxious to cover up grandparent incompetence! Having brought up four active/lively children, I was caught out by how exhausting it was restarting that stuff in my fifties even for *one* small child.

But . . . no doubt despite their young age, grandchildren keep all our brain cells working and remind us what imagination really is. I *love* it. I asked Ava (then five) what games she played with her friends at school break?

"All sorts, Grandpa. Maybe Unicornland or Wrongeland or stuff like that."

At first I wondered if these were some sort of commercial or media inventions but was heartened to hear the ins and outs were created by themselves and explained very matter-of-fact to me that Wrongeland just means everything is the wrong way round and upside down and inside out and big is small etc. (obviously, Grandpa. The largest number is zero and smallest is Infinity!) She quickly realized Grandpa maybe not quite up to this but offered to let me play sometime (she didn't embarrass her/me by pursuing this!).

We maybe all recognize, in retrospect, that small children are sponges for knowledge and particularly the spoken word—care required. Phrases may be repeated and returned when least expected. I realized this early when Ava was just three years old and about to go upstairs in our house. I asked her to carry something up to her bedroom.

"Sorry, Grandpa, my hands are full!"

In the same way children are and always have been children but maybe they are exposed to so much information and come to expect it that it catches us all out. A couple of stories spring to mind from Ava's preschool years.

The kindergarten teacher reflected that it *can* be good to have forthright children who know what they want. She had asked the class if there was anything they might like to learn about? The response was immediate from Ava and her friend Mara.

"Yes, we have a list of things that we *need* to learn about." And they proceeded to reel off all sorts of topics: science, nature, language, etc.

On another occasion the topic was nature. The teacher had a large chart with various marine animals which the children were to name, and it came to Ava's turn. She seemed to be struggling, and the teacher was a bit surprised so she tried to prompt her, suggesting it was something she would have seen before. . ."

"No, Miss I haven't. The tail looks like a grey seal, but the head is more like a harbour seal, and the coat is really like a spotted seal, so I really don't know what it is!" •

George Garrett

George is one of British Columbia's legendary radio reporters, working for CKNW for decades and winning countless awards.

My wife Joan and I have been blessed with four wonderful grandchildren . . . two each from our daughters Linda and Lorrie. Our son Ken never had a chance to have a family. He died in a canoeing accident at age twenty-five. The loss of our son meant that the arrival of grandchildren was even more precious. Joan devoted herself to the babies who seemed to arrive very quickly.

Lorrie and her husband Dave are the proud parents of Lianne, now a schoolteacher (like her mother), and Trevor, a sports enthusiast and all-round good guy.

Linda and her husband Bill honoured our late son by naming their son Kenny, now a broadcast technician and radio host in the Los Angeles area. Kenny was followed by a bright little girl, Mary Paige, who never missed a thing. She is now a maternity ward nurse in the very unit where she was born at a hospital in Vancouver.

The kids grew up so fast we couldn't believe it. Unfortunately, Joan could not enjoy them these past few years because of Alzheimer's. She does not now recognize the children she loved so dearly.

I am happy to say I am very close to all four of my grandchildren. I asked them to write down their thoughts about grandparents. Here they are in the order of their birthdates (which I dare not disclose).

LIANNE WATT—*UVic grad and teacher*

Some of my favourite childhood memories took place with my grandparents. I was fortunate to grow up with four amazing, caring and supportive grandparents. We spent countless days at their houses playing with our cousins and all the fun activities they did with us. It was always special when they came with us for family vacations. We have amazing memories of Disneyland, Palm Springs, and all over British Columbia. One of my proudest moments was having three of my grandparents at my university graduation. There is something so special about the relationship between a grandchild and a grandparent. Grandparents spoil you, support you, take pride in everything you do and love you unconditionally. They also let you have ice cream for dinner.

KENNY FIELD—*Columbia School of Broadcasting graduate, now a broadcast technician and host of his own radio program in Long Beach, California*

Our grandparents are, simply put, the best! Whether it was summer adventures to Cultus Lake, touring around British Columbia, Christmas Eve spent at their house, or listening to Canucks games on the radio and eating sweets until the sun came up, we grandkids were always well looked after. We were always encouraged and supported, learning some important lessons along the way. Some of my fondest memories are with my Ahmey (Eulah Field) and Grandma & Papa (Joan and George Garrett).

MARY PAIGE FIELD—*UVic grad and maternity ward nurse*

It's hard to imagine my childhood without Grandma and Papa. They were so involved from day one. Some of my fondest memories are being picked up from elementary school by Grandma and Papa when my parents were at work. My brother Kenny would excitedly ask, "What's for dinner?" Grandma would always respond with "liver and onions" though that was never actually served. For my thirteenth birthday, G&P took me out for dinner saying I could choose any restaurant I wanted. I picked Costco for chicken strips and fries. On my first and only trip to Saskatchewan, we stayed at the Tropical Inn in North Battleford (where my Grandma was born). It was far from tropical. As a kid I was excited about the indoor pool and water slide that the hotel offered. Unfortunately, there was a water advisory. The pool and slide were out of commission. Our family often talks about Papa and his "Garrett Klutz gene" due to all of the bumps and bruises he has given himself over the years. Although I am not officially a Garrett, I certainly inherited this gene as I am always going up the stairs and bumping into things myself.

TREVOR WATT—*UVic grad, sales rep, and hockey coach*

I have so many great memories of Grandma and Papa as I grew up. Two things that will always stand out are their commitment to my minor sports career and a trip to Palm Desert. Whenever I stepped onto the ice (from age four to eighteen) I would look up into the crowd and see Grandma wrapped in a blanket and Papa talking hockey with other parents in the stands. They always showed interest in my athletic journey, and for this I am forever thankful.

Palm Desert has always been a special place for our entire family. Later, when Grandma was unable to make the trip due to Alzheimer's, I had the opportunity to join Papa and a group of his lifelong friends for two weeks of fun in the sun. What a great trip. Several rounds of golf, cribbage and gin and tonic at happy hour, and countless hours by the pool. The trip coincided with the early stages of Papa writing his book. It was a true honour to get a sneak peek and help him organize his ever-so-cluttered laptop files. Everyone says they have the best grandparents, and I can certainly say that about mine. The lessons I have learned and knowledge I have been able to absorb from such an impressive couple will stay with me for a lifetime. •

Gord Eastwood

Gord was my city editor at the Ottawa Journal *and was a first-rate newsman and great friend. He is now retired in Nova Scotia.*

When our eldest grandson Zac was a two-year-old, he always wanted to be taken outside in his stroller if a garbage truck went by the house. He watched in awe as the truck picked up refuse by the curb. Was it an omen? When he was in college, he drove a Toronto Transit Commission bus to earn a few dollars. When he graduated, he became a Toronto firefighter. Guess what job he has now? He drives the firetruck.

Another grandson, Justin, was with us on a trip to England. For breakfast he discovered Coco Pops and ate a few bowls before we took off for a drive through the Yorkshire Dales. The roads were twisty and hilly, and we hadn't gone very far when the two-year-old threw up all over the backseat. We stopped by a babbling brook to wash him down and clean the car. His clothes were a mess. We drove into the nearest town and stopped at a clothing store. We walked the kid, nude, into the shop and said, "We need clothes for this child."

His naked condition prompted quick service in front of other customers, and we continued our tour with a smartly dressed young boy.

Our teenage granddaughter Paige was left in my care for an afternoon while her mother and grandmother went shopping. This was a fantastic opportunity to tell many of my old war stories to a brand-new audience. Several hours later, when her mother returned, she asked her daughter how she had made out with her grandfather. The granddaughter said she had a great time hearing all these wonderful stories and then gave me the ultimate teenage tribute.

"Grandpa is cool," she said.

When our youngest grandson Josh was about six years old, we took him, his parents, and older brother to a family restaurant in Halifax, Nova Scotia. He announced that he wanted to be a waiter and asked our server if she would show him how to do it. She took him to various tables where they took diners' orders. When they came to our table, Josh politely asked, "What would you like to eat, sir? And you madam?" When he got to his brother, he said "And what'll you have, kid?"

That ended his early career, but he became a server at a steak house while going to college. •

Chris Edwards

Chris is my half-brother who lives in Newcastle, Australia. He has many grandkids and great grandkids. I've lost count.

We regularly used to travel to Sydney on a Sunday afternoon on train to collect three-, then four-year-old, Caspian—with a stentorian voice for his age—and bring him home to stay with Nanna (too chic, modern, and brisk to be called *grandma*) and Pa. On one return journey, Caspian wants to use the toilet, so I dutifully take him, wait outside of the cramped cubicle peeping around the door to see if he had completed his mission with instructions for him to make sure he washes his hands. He finally exits from the cubicle with wet hands and shakes them everywhere. We return to our seat—still kindly left vacant by considerate fellow passengers—and I am just settling down to enjoy the flitting scenery whoosh by and settle into my crossword when, in a voice that stunned, amazed, and eventually amused the travellers, Caspian yelled out, "Pa! I forgot to wipe my bum." •

Peter Ottley

Peter and I have been friends for many years. We play bad golf, talk about soccer a lot, and also talk about our grandkids.

I went to watch my grandson Owen, who was playing football with his local team in an end of season cup final. The venue was unlike their usual local authority pitches that they played on, and came complete with grandstand and was a good setting for the final.

Owen was sixteen years old at the time but had the stature of a twelve-year-old and was the smallest player on the pitch. However, this did not stop him being a little terrier in midfield, with tenacious tackling and a good eye for the right pass to his teammates.

I was very proud of the way he played and thought that he was one of the best players on the pitch. I even overheard this fact being stated by other members in the crowd who were there to support the opposition.

Owen's team won the game 1-0 with the winning goal being scored in the last minute of the game. At the conclusion, Owen came over to see us, and as normal, I leaned forward to give him a hug; however, he stepped back and then offered me his hand to shake.

The unspoken message to grandad: *I am a big boy now.* •

Andria and Mike Gillespie

Andria, Mike, and I have been our friends from Ottawa days. They now live on Protection Island. Andria asked if she could write something about her grandfathers.

Papa Murchison's wooden arm with the black metal hinges hung on the dining room wall of the summer camp that looked out over the St. John River. My favourite story as we sat together on the front camp porch was the one about "The Bear." It seems one day he headed out into the woods behind the camp to do some hunting when a hungry bear came up behind him and grabbed the top of his arm in its big jaws and tore it completely off! However, Papa managed to shoot the bear dead before it ate him up completely. It was a thrilling tale that explained why Papa's right sleeve was always pinned to his shoulder. It wasn't until after he died that I finally learned the truth. You see, both my grandfathers' lives had been shaped by war.

Grampie Murray had a long, deep red valley extending down his leg from just below his knee to just above the ankle. There was a hole in the middle. When I was visiting Saint John, I would help my Grammie remove the bandaging, wash the wound and smear white salve along the raw flesh before rewrapping his leg in gauze. Although he never discussed it, I always knew how Grampie got that horrible injury.

No, Grampie was a man of few words, but his hugs were warm and genuine. I especially took great pride in rolling him the perfect cigarette. It would involve sitting at the dining room table in front of a metal contraption where I'd stuff tobacco from a green tin into white paper and roll it as tightly as possible to make a good firm cylinder. Finally, I'd bring down the metal arm that had two sharp blades and voila—three identical cigarettes at once! Every year when I visited him in Saint John it took a few "goes" to get the tobacco good and tight to Grampie's satisfaction. But I loved to see the glint in his eyes and the big smile when I got it just right.

Growing up, I was fortunate to have the deep love of all four of my grandparents. My grandmothers had their own interesting life stories, but luckily they didn't fight in a war. •

Mike McRanor

Mike is former executive editor of the Vancouver Sun. *He is a larger-than-life Scotsman and one helluva journalist, with a rough-tough exterior and a heart of gold.*

My friend Vic Wittenberg said of his grandchildren: "If I'd known how much fun they are, I'd have had 'em first."

His affection was profound: when his son's family moved to California, Vic sold his Vancouver electrical business and joined them.

Son Graeme and partner Tina presented us with grandson London McRanor on August 29, 2008, the day before a holiday flight to Maui; I was so smitten that I proposed cancelling the trip. London is now eleven, wife Pat and I having shared daycare from infancy with the maternal Johnston family.

He sat on my lap while showing an early interest in reading, skipped the so-called terrible twos, and showed no desire to kick, throw, or hit a ball as we dallied on the walk home from kindergarten. Primary school required afternoon pickup, and that's where he blossomed. By request, Bieber replaced Beethoven on the radio, and between music and periods of contemplation, he would chatter with brushfire intensity—quip, question and observation tumbling randomly, as in this sample as a seven-year-old:

"The most fascinating thing in the world is your mind. And Lego. There's no future in broccoli. Why do some people fall when they feel love—it makes me want to dance. Some solutions are just as hard as the problems, don't you think? I haven't fallen asleep yet, but I'm already bored."

Reluctant to acknowledge error, he'd often counter with a plausible argument that nevertheless suggested he could be right. He dazzled with insight, solved for me the riddle of the smartphone, and declined the editing hand of the veteran journalist, insisting that nothing be changed in a school essay that began:

"The watermelon is truly an unbelievably extravagant fruit of hope and peace. The rind and flesh are edible but for some reason people do not eat the rind. How could you waste such food? It's unbelievable! It's inhumane!"

Recently, London and family moved to White Rock, severing a decade-long daily contact. I didn't follow, but I see him regularly when, in a sense, he restores the melody to a long lyric of attachment. Mostly, he remains a rainbow potted in my heart, etched by the sweetest of his sentiments: "If I knew you as a child, I would have been your friend."

London unbound: "Sometime in my life I'm going to wear an eyepatch. How about I change my surname to England? My favourite thing is your voice. When you speak to me it sounds like love. Except when you're angry. Then I like your hair more. When I say 'I love you' pretend I've never told you before, so it feels brand new? Okay? I wonder why you forget? I think it's because your body forgot but your memory remembered. You know how vampires talk? It's like speaking French except they are vampires. There's some days you want to share your popcorn. And some days you don't. Today I'm sharing. That's all you need to know. What I'm about to tell you is very rare. It's only happened to me twice in my life . . . and I'm only seven. I'm not the type of kid to stay still. My body was made to move." •

Bob Stall

Bob is a legendary Canadian journalist. He has worked for Weekend *magazine and written beautiful—and funny—columns for the* Province *newspaper.*

Thank you, Greta Thunberg and your millions of cohorts, for milling and yelling and waking me up.

I am a seventy-seven-year-old, white, anglo North American male. I am too old and comfortable, lazy and slow to rouse. I am what is wrong with the world today.

I have been a Canadian journalist for almost sixty years and have never written about climate change or the increasingly imminent doom of this planet for which my generation remains in stupefying denial of both our culpability and responsibility to fix it.

If we are like too many we elect or select to work for, we are worse than lazy and slow. We are greedy, venal, and corrupt. We continue to dig, suck, belch, and emit because to abate would reduce the short-term profits of the most bloated of our fat cats.

Greta, you and the kids have ensured that henceforth I will think, act, and vote as green as I can. Down the road and over the horizon, I vow to keep my eyes on David, Zev, Olive, and Waylon who are my grandchildren. They're the ones for whom I belatedly fear because for too long I neglected to think of them. They're the ones who will suffer from our sins of emission.

For too long, billions like me forgot what brought us here. It was this verdant planet, Mother Earth, who gave birth and worth to us. She nurtured and grew us, evolving her brood. Always she knew us and gave us our food, grass, and trees for shade and shelter and ships to sail and anchor. We never had to help her, and rarely did we thank her.

Instead we ignored and then we abused her, poisoned her skies and seas, raped her soil and ripped the trees, melted the ice and twisted the tides until flames roared and species died. Very late, some of her children awoke, their voices at first swamped in the swill of the spills, choked in the smoke, and buried in the ashes of the fires of the liars and deniers.

But keep yelling to be heard, dear Greta, for the sake of all our grandchildren. Thank you for being there for them. •

Roger Hope

Roger is a veteran cameraman for Global News *in Vancouver. His wife, Deborra Hope, is well-known as the former anchor at BCTV, and later Global. Roger and I are close friends. We both play music and are writing a musical.*

My granddaughter Ella and I were driving in my car the other day, listening to some songs that I've written for a musical that I'm writing with my friend Ian.

Now, I have three daughters. It's my joy, and my curse. A hat trick you might say. Ella is my first granddaughter with my oldest daughter. She's eight.

My two younger daughters were helping, by singing demos of the songs I've written. Ella and I were listening to her aunties sing when she turned to me.

"Why isn't my mother singing one of the songs?"

Why, indeed.

That night I gave Ella, who was in the front seat, and her family a ride to dinner. After playing the songs for my oldest daughter, I turned and asked if she'd like to sing one?

"I'd love to," she said.

Ella and I glanced at each other, but never said a word.

It was at that moment, I realized, that my eight-year-old granddaughter Ella was smarter than I am.

My grandson Joe is three years old and is totally infatuated with airplanes. You've never seen anything like it. My father, Joe's great-grandpa, was a pilot in the Second World War with the RAF. He did two tours of duty, crashed three times, and always walked away without a scratch.

One afternoon, I was sitting on the couch with Joe's dad telling him the story of how *my* dad kept running out of gas when flying. Joe was sitting between us with his head turning from side to side following the conversation intently.

After I'd finished the story, Joe sat quietly for a few minutes, then looked up at me with great concern.

"Ga ta on."

I said, "Pardon me, Joe what's that?

"Gat ta on."

"What?"

"Ga Ta Ton!"

Suddenly I realized, he was saying, "Gas Station."

Joe had figured out what Great-Grandpa needed to do to avoid crashing his airplane. Why, fill up with gas at the gas station of course. Out of the mouths of babes. We were all astonished.

On Halloween, Joe wore a pilot's costume. The kids in the neighborhood followed him from door to door. My daughter thinks it's because he was wearing a uniform.

I believe that sometimes, people know at a very young age what they want to be, and if their parents recognize it, and encourage it, that the sky's the limit. •

Chester Grant

Chester is a great journalist, and lovely man, working on the assignment desk at BCTV News and Global for many years. He told me this story about his grandson Malcolm, and I loved it. He had his daughter-in-law Candace provide the official version.

On a typical Port Coquitlam rainy afternoon, I (Mom) arrive at the Hyde Creek Recreation Centre to pick up my four-year-old son, Malcolm, from a recreation class. Like any four-year-old, he loves to goof around and run as fast as possible, sometimes showing off how similar he is to "The Flash." And like any typical Mom, I enrolled him into this class to a) burn off energy, b) have some Mom alone time, and c) it's naptime . . . and the kid isn't gonna nap!

The door opens, and the instructor is there—a lovely, patient lady—and she catches my eye.

"I have something to tell you once Malcolm has his shoes on."

Oh no. What happened now? Did he have a run in with another child? Bracing myself (a bit), I walk up to the instructor.

"So, a few weeks ago," she says, "when the class first started, I laid some ground rules with the kids—the usual stuff. And last week, I asked the class if anybody remembered some of the rules we talked about the previous week? and Malcolm said, 'Yeah, not to say bad words, like stupid . . . and fuck.'"

I couldn't help but laugh, and I've been laughing all week, ever since it happened."

I smile with the teacher, have a laugh, and thank her for telling me. Not really want you want to hear, but it was good-natured, innocent, and well-received, so I guess that is a win for any Mom?! •

Randy McHale

Randy was executive producer of BCTV's News Hour *and then Global's* News Hour. *We play golf (do you detect a pattern here?) and laugh a lot. He's one of the funniest people I know.*

When our first grandchild was very young, he somehow decided that he liked Batman. None of us was even sure how he knew about the Dark Knight, but he made it very clear that he wanted to know more.

As it happened, we owned a large collection of movies at the time. And sure enough, it included one of the early Batman movies. I can't remember whose bright idea this was, but I found myself sitting in the TV room with young Bronson, the video cued up and ready to go. There were to be no scenes of violence, no adult themes at all—I had promised my daughter that. And I had already mapped out the suitable bits and sharpened my non-existent skills with the remote. What could possibly go wrong? And anyway, hadn't I already armoured the poor child with my great clanging philosophy that violence is never the answer?

And so it was, in a deep sweat, that I pressed PLAY at the very moment that my grandson put a reassuring hand on my arm.

"Don't be afraid, Papa, it's only a movie."

He was three. •

Afterword

It all started with a pair of red boots. I was a young student at journalism college near London, heading into the centre of town at lunchtime, when ahead of me was a young long-haired woman in red boots—and wearing a mini skirt, this being the late sixties.

I followed those boots, caught up with the fellow journalism student, and instantly fell in love with her. With her smile. Her eyes. Her laugh. Her everything.

If memory serves, I had my own long hair under a bandana and was wearing a Che Guevara T-shirt, so I wasn't exactly a catch. She didn't seem to mind. We walked together into the centre of town and have walked together through life ever since.

It feels like fate. Because I followed first those red boots and then my heart, we have four kids and three grandchildren—with a fourth grandchild on the way.

Our son Tim and his partner Jacy are expecting their first grandchild this summer. We call him (or her) TJ for now—the parents' initials—though at the time of writing he (or she) is a big, beautiful bump. They say they'd like more than one. Life just keeps getting better.

We are, as Cat Stevens once sang, only dancing on this world for a short while, and as you get older, you're more aware of that with every passing, precious second. You savour every stolen moment.

I also, more than ever, appreciate the randomness and the magic of life. We are here, not just because Beth and I crossed paths dressed in our hippie garb, but also because two other people met centuries

181

and centuries ago. And then two other people met and got together. And then two others.

Destiny? Luck? Who knows? We are lucky to have got to dance this dance. All of us. But I do know that dancing, for even a short while, with my grandchildren has been a joy almost beyond measure. I hadn't imagined it could be this wondrous just to share this short time with them. Even when they screamed. Or sprayed me with water. Or wrecked my back.

Being a grandfather helps you remember your inner child.

Here's some of the things I learned in the trenches of modern grandparenthood:

Children are beautiful. Oh, sure, we mess them up. We put silly things into their heads as they grow older, and they lose that wonderful innocence. But there's nothing as indescribably perfect as a granddaughter laughing and smiling and holding your hand.

Kids are wiser than you think. When Mayana told me she'd figured out the difference between adults and kids (adults talk, kids play), she was on the money.

Adults should play more. And skip along the street. And try and miss the lines on the sidewalk. And sing. And sometimes go *wheeeee* ... as they run along a country path. Dance like nobody's watching? Live like nobody's watching.

Grandkids don't whine so much when their parents aren't around.

Don't talk to children as if they're babies. Or they'll act like babies.

Grandkids are useless at hide and seek.

You don't need expensive trips. Mostly, you need a puddle.

Try not to shout "Shit" at the top of your voice or "Asshole" to another driver when you're in the car with your granddaughter. Not if you don't want to get told off.

"Grandad, can you help me take my shoes off." That's music to my soul.

A tub full of bubbles before bedtime is better than watching an Oscar-winning comedy.

Try and keep up. "Come on, Grandad. Come on."

Kids say the neatest things. "Grandad, my feet are sweating."

Enjoy every moment. Even the bad ones. You'll soon forget them. And remember the rest.

They will too.

You want to preserve your grandchildren in time . . . to stay forever at maybe three or four years old. You want these moments to stay exactly like this. But then you want to live long enough to watch them graduate. Maybe get married (if they want to) . . . and have kids—your great-grandchildren. Yikes!

Don't be a grumpy old man around your grandkids. Do you want them to call you Grumpa?

Make up stories.

Octopuses in the aquarium can be scary when you're three years old.

Sing lullabies.

Just sing.

Though I thank my ancestors for enabling me to be here, I don't dwell on family trees, so much, but on the future. I imagine my grandchildren having their own lives, their own experiences, their own victories and defeats, and though I won't be here to share all of those experiences, they should know how much joy they have brought me. Just as my kids did.

In its infancy, this book was simply *My Summer with Mayana*. Because she insinuated herself into my heart. Then Emma and Linden came along, and I wrote even more. Now another grandchild, and another chapter, is yet to come. I am happy beyond words.

This is my love letter to them. •

Acknowledgements

First, I'd like to thank my family for putting up with me. To my wife Beth, who has been supportive throughout my journalistic career, through more ups than downs, but also for sharing this adventure of life.

To my four children Amy, Jani, Tim, and Paul who continue to amaze and delight me and make me proud. The journey with them has been, well, wonderful (my favourite word, apparently). They're all a lot smarter than me and better-looking, but I still love them.

And thanks too—obviously—to my grandchildren for giving me inspiration every day and endless laughter.

This book began as an idea many years ago when staying at Discovery Islands Lodge on Quadra Island, run by our friends Ralph and Lani Keller. I had left full-time journalism and was happily sitting on a dock by the ocean, looking up at the mountains. I was singing on my guitar to Mayana as she giggled along and realized how much unabashed joy I derived from being a new grandfather. I'd originally thought of writing a book about some of my funnier journalism memories, but decided I'd do this one first.

My thanks also to the friends, relatives, and colleagues who contributed their grandfatherly vignettes. We are now a cult.

 My thanks to the Victoria *Times Colonist* and *Vancouver Sun*, for allowing me to dig into their archives to retrieve some old columns, though in the end we cut just about all of those bits out. Every writer needs a good editor.

My editor at Heritage House, Warren Layberry, has been superb, and I thank him for his counsel, guidance, and professionalism. Thanks also to Lara Kordic, Nandini Thaker, and Leslie Kenny for their support and patience.

And finally, my thanks to Jack Knox, the super-funny Victoria *Times Colonist* columnist who encouraged me to publish this book. Blame him. •

STOP THE PRESS!

That's an old newspaper term for when presses were stopped to insert late-breaking news.

Well, our hold-the-back-page news is that as this book was being readied for the printers, our fourth grandchild, Summer, was born in North Vancouver! In the summer, of course! She is adorable, with blonde hair, big eyes, and tiny, perfect hands. We will play piano together. I'll teach her *Chopsticks*.

Mum Jacy, Dad Tim, and Summer are all doing fine.

Now that's some late-breaking *good* news.

The story continues . . . •

About the Author

Ian Haysom is a lifelong journalist who has worked in newspapers, television, and online. He has been a reporter, feature writer, music writer, film critic, correspondent, city editor, and columnist. He was editor-in-chief of two of Canada's largest newspapers, the *Vancouver Province* and the *Vancouver Sun*. He started his career in England, worked in Fleet Street, but spent most of his journalistic career in, first, eastern Canada on the *Hamilton Spectator, Ottawa Journal,* and *Ottawa Citizen,* then British Columbia. He later moved to television news, as the news director for BCTV News, CHEK News in Victoria, and Global News in Vancouver. His writing has appeared in most major Canadian newspapers over the past four decades. •